# Lecture Notes in Computer Science

Commenced Publication in 1973
Founding and Former Series Editors:
Gerhard Goos, Juris Hartmanis, and Jan van Leeuwen

Patrick Eugster (Ed.)

# Object-Oriented Technology

## ECOOP 2008 Workshop Reader

ECOOP 2008 Workshops
Paphos, Cyprus, July 7-11, 2008
Final Reports

 Springer

Volume Editor

Patrick Eugster
Purdue University
Department of Computer Science
305 North University Street, West Lafayette, IN 47907, USA
E-mail: p@cs.purdue.edu

Library of Congress Control Number: Applied for

CR Subject Classification (1998): D.1.5, D.2.1, D.2.2, D.2.3, D.3.2, F.3.3

LNCS Sublibrary: SL 2 – Programming and Software Engineering

ISSN        0302-9743
ISBN-10     3-642-02046-1 Springer Berlin Heidelberg New York
ISBN-13     978-3-642-02046-9 Springer Berlin Heidelberg New York

springer.com

© Springer-Verlag Berlin Heidelberg 2009
Printed in Germany

Typesetting: Camera-ready by author, data conversion by Scientific Publishing Services, Chennai, India
Printed on acid-free paper      SPIN: 12663040      06/3180      5 4 3 2 1 0

# Preface

This volume presents the reports from the workshops held in conjunction with the European Conference on Object-Oriented Programming (ECOOP 2008), taking place in its 22nd edition at Coral Beach in Paphos, Cyprus, July 7–11 2008.

As is customary, the workshops introduced the conference, taking place on the first two days (July 7 and July 8 2008) prior to the main technical track. The workshops were first chosen through a rigorous process with stringent selection criteria, carried out by the members of the Workshop Selection Committee. This volume collects reports from the resulting high-quality workshops. The topics covered span areas related to object-oriented programming and technology, such as programming languages, aspects, parallel computing, formal techniques, software engineering, tools, and applications. By summarizing the outcome of these workshops, this volume provides readers with a comprehensive set of pointers into current trends and issues of intense investigation and debate in the field of object-oriented technology. Following the tradition, the individual workshop reports summarize the workshop goals, before providing an overview of the presentations and sometimes also a summary of the issues and findings of debates fueled by the presentations. Some reports may also include a list of participants or contributed position papers. Several of the reports also contain a list of references to relevant publications and websites, including the workshop home page which usually offers the contributed position papers for download and may present further material.

This workshop reader is the result of the contributions of many people to whom we would like to express our gratitude, namely, all submitters of workshop proposals and workshop contributions, the workshop organizers, the co-authors of the reports, and the participants who contributed to the workshops directly through presentations and discussions.

We are also very grateful to the members of the Workshop Selection Committee for devoting time and effort to ensure a workshop program covering a broad range of exciting and timely topics and living up to the high-quality standards of the ECOOP conference series. Last but not least, we wish to thank the local organizers for their contributions toward the success of the workshop program at ECOOP 2008.

November 2008                                                    Patrick Eugster

# Organization

ECOOP 2008 was organized by the Department of Computer Science of the University of Cyprus, under the auspices of AITO (Association Internationale pour les Technologies Objets), and in cooperation with ACM SIGPLAN and SIGSOFT.

## Workshop Organization

Workshop Co-chairs

Patrick Eugster(Purdue University, USA)
Costas Pattichis (University of Cyprus, Cyprus)

## Workshop Selection Committee

Patrick Eugster          Purdue University, USA
Benoit Garbinato       University of Lausanne, Switzerland
Peter Müller              ETH Zurich, Switzerland
Costas Pattichis        University of Cyprus, Cyprus
Friedrich Steimann     Fernuniversität Hagen, Germany

## Sponsoring Organizations

### Gold

### Silver

# Table of Contents

## ECOOP 2008 Workshops: Final Reports

# Lisp

## Report on the 5th Workshop ELW at ECOOP 2008

Didier Verna[1], Charlotte Herzeel[2], Christophe Rhodes[3], and Hans Hübner[4]

[1] EPITA Research and Development Laboratory, Paris, France
[2] Programming Technology Lab, Vrije Universiteit, Brussel, Belgium
[3] Goldsmiths College, University of London, United Kingdom
[4] Berlin, Germany

**Abstract.** This report covers the activities of the 5th European Lisp and Scheme Workshop. We introduce the motivation for a workshop focusing on languages in the Lisp family, and mention relevant organizational aspects. We summarize the presentations and discussions, including Mark Tarver and Rich Hickey's keynote talks, and provide pointers to related work and events.

## 1 Introduction

Lisp is one of the eldest computer languages still in use today. In the decades of its existence, Lisp has been a fruitful basis for language design experiments as well as the preferred implementation language for applications in diverse fields.

The structure of Lisp makes it easy to extend the language or even to implement entirely new dialects without starting from scratch. Common Lisp, with the Common Lisp Object System (CLOS), was the first object-oriented programming language to receive an ANSI standard and retains the most complete and advanced object system of any programming language, while influencing many other object-oriented programming languages that followed.

It is clear today that Lisp is gaining momentum: there is a steadily growing interest in Lisp itself, with numerous user groups in existence worldwide, and in Lisp's meta-programming notions which are being transferred to other languages, as for example in Aspect-Oriented Programming, support for Domain-Specific Languages, and so on.

The theme of the workshop held at ECOOP 2008 was intentionally broad, aimed at encouraging lively discussion between researchers proposing new ideas and practitioners reporting on their experience with the strengths and limitations of current Lisp technologies, with the intent to address the near-future evolution of Lisp-based languages and Object-Oriented techniques in research, industry and education.

## 2 Organization

This section describes the organizational aspects of the workshop. The submitted papers and workshop slides can be found at the workshop's website:

P. Eugster (Ed.): ECOOP 2008 Workshop Reader, LNCS 5475, pp. 1–6, 2009.

`http://elw2008.bknr.net/home`. Note that we now have a centralized website archiving all previous occurrences of the workshop: `http://elw.bknr.net/`

## 2.1  Organizers

Didier Verna, EPITA Research and Development Laboratory, Paris, France, *Contact Organizer*, `didier@lrde.epita.fr`

Charlotte Herzeel, Programming Technology Lab, Vrije Universiteit, Brussel, Belgium, `charlotte.herzeel@vub.ac.be`

Christophe Rhodes, Goldsmiths College, University of London, United Kingdom, `c.rhodes@gold.ac.uk`

Hans Hübner, Berlin, Germany, `hans.huebner@gmail.com` (website)

## 2.2  Sponsors

Organizing the workshop would not have been possible without the help of our sponsors: LispWorks Ltd[1], Franz Inc[2], the Association of Lisp Users[3], and EPITA[4].

## 2.3  Call for Participation

> ... please don't assume Lisp is only useful for Animation and Graphics, AI, Bio-informatics, B2B and E-Commerce, Data Mining, EDA/Semiconductor applications, Expert Systems, Finance, Intelligent Agents, Knowledge Management, Mechanical CAD, Modeling and Simulation, Natural Language, Optimization, Research, Risk Analysis, Scheduling, Telecom, and Web Authoring just because these are the only things they happened to list.
>
> - Kent Pitman[5]

Potential attendees were invited to contribute a long paper (10 pages) presenting scientific or empirical results about Lisp- and Scheme-based uses or new approaches for software engineering purposes; a short essay (5 pages) defending a position about where research and practice based on Lisp should be heading in the near future; or a proposal for a breakout group describing an agenda for discussion.

Suggested topics for presented papers included: new language features or abstractions; experience reports or case studies; protocol meta-programming and libraries; educational approaches; software evolution; development aids; persistent systems; dynamic optimization; implementation techniques; innovative applications; hardware support for lisp systems; macro-, reflective-, meta- and/or rule-based development approaches; and aspect-oriented, domain-oriented and generative programming.

## 2.4   Format

The workshop was held on the first day of ECOOP 2008. After a short opening by Didier Verna, Mark Tarver gave a keynote entitled "Lisp for the 21st Century". The workshop continued with three of the four accepted papers (described in section 3). In the afternoon, a second keynote was given by Rich Hickey: "A Detailed Look at the Lisp Nature of Clojure", and was followed by the last of the four accepted papers. Didier Verna then concluded the workshop.

# 3   Presentations

There were four accepted papers for presentation at the workshop, along with the invited keynote talks from Mark Tarver and Rich Hickey.

## 3.1   Invited Speakers

### Lisp for the 21st Century   Mark Tarver

> As Lisp reaches its 50th anniversary, the talk looked at some of the reasons why Lisp has not found a wider acceptance amongst the programming community. Part of the reasons lie in a vicious cycle between education and industry within which Lisp is trapped. One solution is the L21 project – to produce a rationalized and revised update of Lisp for the C21. Qi[6] fits many of the constraints of the L21 project. The talk concluded on what needs to be done within Qi and the Lisp world to bring Lisp to the center stage.

### A Detailed Look at the Lisp Nature of Clojure   Rich Hickey

> The small essential core of Lisp makes dialects easy to define and implement. Most dialects are viewed skeptically by the community, as their features can be realized via the extensibility mechanisms of Scheme or Common Lisp. However, functional programming, interoperability, extensibility and concurrency objectives call for different decisions at many Lisp design points. Meeting those objectives in a Lisp dialect testifies to the continued vitality of the Lisp idea. This talk provided a rationale for Clojure[7] as a substantive and unique dialect of Lisp, and details of its design and implementation on the JVM.

## 3.2   Accepted Papers

**Software Abstractions for Description Logic Systems.** Michael Wessel and Ralf Möller, Hamburg University of Technology, Institute for Software, Technology, and Systems (STS) Hamburg, Germany

The basics of description logics[8] and tableau provers for reasoning with them were explained. The implementation of tableau provers is a complicated matter and demanding from a software engineering point of view. Their implementation in Common Lisp was presented and discussed. Some novel software abstractions for description logic system construction were also motivated and introduced. The MIDELORA toolkit / framework was presented as a grounding example system for these ideas.

**Using Data Parallelism in Lisp for Implementing a Quantum Simulator.** Leonardo Uribe, Pascal Costanza, Charlotte Herzeel, Theo D'Hondt Programming Technology Lab Vrije Universiteit Brussel, Belgium

This paper described two implementations of QLisp (a Lisp extension to simulate quantum computations) in two different data-parallel extensions of Lisp: *Lisp[9] and Paralation Lisp[10]. First, the basic concepts of the languages and the quantum simulator were explained. Then, the porting process was described and a comparative evaluation of the two implementations was made. It was shown that data parallel languages are well suited for parallelizing QLisp. Also, in the porting process, the authors discovered some non-obvious differences between the different data parallel languages.

**Adaptive Libraries and Interactive Code Generation for Common Lisp.** Geoff Wozniak, Mark Daley and Stephen Watt, Department of Computer Science / Biology, University of Western Ontario, London, Canada

The authors illustrated the use of a library for an abstract data type whose instances represent the union of various data types and are specialized based on their use. The ADT can be used for a single collection of data that is viewed in different ways in the program. A behavioral analysis determines a specialized type that reflects the use of the data in the program, as well as generating code to define and use the type. The code generation is interactive in that it works in conjunction with a text editor to determine where in the program the specializations are to take place. The authors presented this as a technique for using evaluation to disambiguate code representing many programs and argued that it is useful for design exploration.

`make-method-lambda` **Considered Harmful.** Pascal Costanza and Charlotte Herzeel Vrije Universiteit Brussel, Belgium

The CLOS Metaobject Protocol[11] (CLOS MOP) is a specification of how major building blocks of CLOS are implemented in terms of CLOS itself. This enables programmers to subclass meta-level classes and define meta-level state and behavior in an incremental fashion. The benefits of such a meta-level architecture for object systems in general and CLOS in particular are well documented. However, some parts of the CLOS MOP are underspecified or impractical to use. The authors discussed a particular dark corner of the CLOS MOP, the meta-level function `make-method-lambda`, whose purpose is to influence the expansion, and thus the semantics, of `defmethod` forms. They also made concrete suggestions for an alternative design for achieving the functionality that `make-method-lambda` provides, without any of its drawbacks.

## 4  Discussion

The 5th European Lisp Workshop was the third notable Lisp event in the year 2008: within a one month interval, both the European Common Lisp Meeting (Amsterdam, April 20) and the First European Lisp Symposium (Bordeaux, May 22–23) gathered an important number of contributions and a large audience. Given this context, it was quite a challenge to organize *yet* another Lisp manifestation within the same period of time, but we succeeded: ELW'08 featured two invited keynote speakers on very "hot" topics, and four high-quality scientific contributions.

Pessimists would probably qualify this occurrence of the workshop as a "small" one: the audience was about half of what is usually expected. That was actually the case for the whole ECOOP conference, so the workshop was only affected by the same lack of audience as the rest of the conference. On the other hand, there were very clear signs that Lisp continues to regain importance. During the main conference (not even talking about the Dynamic Languages Symposium), the name "Lisp" was mentioned several times by authors explicitly acknowledging the Lisp heritage. To our knowledge, this had not happened in the past few years at ECOOP. Another important sign was that in spite of the small size of the conference, the totality of one of our sponsor's flyers and evaluation CDs was gone in a morning.

For all of these reasons, we think that there is no place for pessimism. The fact that we were able to successfully organize three Lisp events in less than 4 months is a very clear sign that the European Lisp community is not only active, but also attracting new people every day, which is also confirmed by the wide range of applications demonstrated in the workshop's accepted papers.

Along with the lines of being popular again, our two invited speakers gave interesting while diverging views on how to reach that goal. According to Mark Tarver, one way to make Lisp (specifically Common Lisp) popular again is to fill its gaps in matters of practicality and missing features from the pure functional world, like static typing. Rich Hickey, on the other hand, develops a new Lisp-based language on top of the JVM, in the hope that people will gradually come to like it (meaning come to like the features of Lisp, without necessarily knowing that it is a Lisp in the first place), and all of this while staying in an environment that feels like home. These two approaches are very interesting because when put side-by-side, they look quite complementary.

## 5   Related Events

There is an increasing scope for meetings organized around the broad theme of Computer Science and Lisp technology. As mentioned previously, the fifth European Lisp Workshop was the third Lisp event in a row, within a period of a few months. 2009 will be a year full of Lisp event as well. Most notably:

- The International Lisp Conference will be held in Cambridge and celebrate Lisp's 50th anniversary.
- Given the success of the first European Lisp Symposium, the experience will be reconducted in Milan, Italy, and the symposium team is now organized in a steering committee.
- We are also confident that the European Lisp Workshop will continue to be held as a satellite of ECOOP.

Meanwhile, Lisp user groups continue to thrive throughout the world, with frequent meetings of varying levels of formality.

## References

1. Sponsor (LispWorks Ltd.), http://www.lispworks.com/
2. Sponsor (Franz Inc.), http://www.franz.com/
3. Sponsor (ALU), http://www.alu.org/alu/home
4. Sponsor (EPITA), http://www.epita.fr/
5. Pitman, K.: Re: More lisp (2001),
   http://interviews.slashdot.org/comments.pl?sid=23357&cid=2543265
6. Tarver, M.: Qi, http://www.lambdassociates.org/
7. Hickey, R.: Clojure, http://clojure.org/
8. Baader, F., Calvanese, D., McGuinness, D., Nardi, D., Patel-Schneider, P.: The Description Logic Handbook - Theory, Implementation and Applications. Cambridge University Press, Cambridge (2003)
9. Meglicki, Z.: The CM5 *Lisp Course, Centre for Information Science Research – The Australian National University (1994)
10. Steele, G., Hillis, D.: Connection machine lisp: Fine-grained parallel symbolic processing. In: Proceedings of the 1986 ACM Conference on LISP and Functional Programming, pp. 279–297. ACM, New York (1986)
11. Kiczales, G.J., des Rivières, J., Bobrow, D.G.: The Art of the Metaobject Protocol. MIT Press, Cambridge (1991)

# Multiparadigm Programming in Object-Oriented Languages: Current Research
## Report on the Workshop MPOOL'08 at ECOOP 2008

Jörg Striegnitz[1] and Kei Davis[2]

[1] University Of Applied Sciences Regensburg 93053 Regensburg, Germany
joerg.striegnitz@informtik.fh-regensburg.de
http://homepages.fh-regensburg.de/striegnitz/people/striegnitz.html
[2] Los Alamos National Laboratory, Los Alamos, NM 87545, USA
kei.davis@lanl.gov
http://www.ccs3.lanl.gov/~kei.html

**Abstract.** While OO has become ubiquitously employed for design, implementation, and even conceptualization, many practitioners recognize the concomitant need for other programming paradigms according to problem domain. Nevertheless, the choice of a programming paradigm is strongly influenced by the supporting programming language facilities. In turn, choice of programming language is usually highly constrained by practical considerations.

We seek answers to the question of how to address the need for other programming paradigms, or even domain specific languages, in the general context of OO languages.

It is clear that this field is active and fluid: novel, disparate approaches and techniques are still being discovered or invented, and this very novelty adds a significant element of intellectual entertainment. This article describes the cross section of research efforts reported at the workshop on Multiparadigm Programming in Object-Oriented Languages held at the 2008 European Conference on Object-Oriented Programming.

## 1 Introduction

While OO has become ubiquitously employed for design, implementation, and even conceptualization, many practitioners recognize the concomitant need for other programming paradigms according to problem domain. We seek answers to the question of how to address the need for other programming paradigms—or even domain specific languages—in the general context of OO languages.

Can OO programming languages effectively support other programming paradigms or the embedding of other languages? The answer seems to be affirmative, at least for some paradigms. For example, significant progress has been made for the case of functional programming in C++.

Additionally, several efforts have been made to integrate support for other paradigms as a front-end for OO languages (the Pizza language, extending Java, is a well-known example).

P. Eugster (Ed.): ECOOP 2008 Workshop Reader, LNCS 5475, pp. 7–17, 2009.

The object-oriented paradigm is in fact well suited to implementation of, and extension to include, other programming paradigms. Our previous years' MPOOL workshops at ECOOP'01, ECOOP'02, OOPSLA'03, ECOOP'04, ECOOP'07 and OOPSLA'05, and the DP-COOL workshop (Declarative Programming in the Context of Object-Oriented Languages) at PLI'03, bore out our hypothesis that there are many such efforts extant, including theoretical treatments, language implementations, practical (application) implementations, even long-extant (Budd) and new (Van Roy) textbooks on multiparadigm programming, though these texts are not specific to the embedding of other paradigms in an OO language.

As in the past the call for contributions generated sufficient response that a mild deselection process was required to maintain relevance, focus, and quality. This process was performed by the organizers who are recognized experts in the field. At the workshop about half of the time was used for presentation, the other half for discussion. This year we had presenters from academia, government laboratories, the public sector, and private industry.

The home page for MPOOL'08, including the archive of papers and presentations, is

http://homepages.fh-regensburg.de/~mpool/mpool08/programme.html

## 2    Presentations

Here we provide synopses of the contributions.

### 2.1    A Calculus of Evolving Objects (Mariangiola Dezani-Ciancaglini, Paola Giannini and Oscar Nierstrasz)

There has been a recent re-emergence of interest in dynamic programming languages and the development of more dynamic features for mainstream languages such as Java. Increasing numbers of applications require the ability for configurations and even system behaviour to evolve at run-time. Furthermore, behaviour may be context-dependent, and may need to adapt to the run-time platform, the end user, service availability, or any number of environmental attributes. To support these highly dynamic applications, programming languages need to support a range of different object models, paradigms and language features.

Multi-dimensional dispatch is one example of a such a feature – instead of dispatching purely on the receiver of a message, the behavior of an object might depend on the sender, or even on contextual information such as the deployment platform, available services, desired quality of service, available versions of components, or even the time of day. Another example is the use of fine-grained components, such as traits, to statically or even dynamically extend the behaviour of classes. These and other mechanisms entail the need for specialized lookup mechanisms to adapt the behaviour of objects, even at run-time.

This paper presents an original calculus in which objects can adapt their behaviour at run-time. Both objects and environments are represented by first-class mappings between variables and values. Message sends are dynamically resolved to method calls. Variables may be dynamically bound, making it possible to model a variety of dynamic mechanisms within the same calculus. Despite the highly dynamic nature of the calculus, safety properties are assured by a type assignment system.

## 2.2 First Class Relationships for OO Languages (Stephen Nelson, David J. Pearce, and James Noble)

Relationships have been an essential component of OO design since the 90s but mainstream OO languages still do not support rst-class relationships. This requires programmers to implement relationships in an ad-hoc fashion which results in unnecessarily complex code. Rather than simply tacking on relationship support to existing language models we propose that existing language models should be re-factored to support relationships as a primary metaphor. We have developed a set of requirements with which to identify good relationship models, and used these requirements to develop a new, three-layered model for the ob ject-oriented paradigm which focuses on relationships rather than objects. In addition, we present a prototype language based on this model. Our approach offers benefits such as improved traceability between design and implementation, reduced boilerplate code, better program understanding by programmers, and the opportunity for better paradigm integration between object-oriented programs and the relational databases prevalent in modern systems.

## 2.3 Object State Querying for Optimisation (David J. Pearce and James Noble)

The Java Query Language (JQL) provides a better separation between interface and implementation than more traditional object-oriented languages. JQL allows the system to optimise code across interface boundaries in sophisticated ways, relieving the programmer from the burden of doing this by hand. The key techniques employed are caching and incrementalisation; these allow previously computed values to be cached automatically for quick retrieval later on. In our case, the values in question represent subsets of collections. Furthermore, during execution, if these collections are changed in some way, the JQL system automatically updates their cached values to reflect the new program state. An interesting observation is that such optimisations are prevalent in the database community, but have yet to make their way into main-stream programming.

## 2.4 Semantics-Driven Genericity: A Sequel to the Static C++ Object-Oriented Programming Paradigm (SCOOP 2) (Thierry Geraud and Roland Levillain)

Classical (unbounded) genericity in C++03 [1] defines the interactions between generic data types and algorithms in terms of concepts [2]. Concepts define the requirements over a type (or a parameter) by expressing constraints on its methods and dependent types (typedefs). The upcoming C++0x standard will promote concepts from abstract entities (not directly enforced by the tools) to language constructs, enabling compilers and tools to perform additional checks on generic constructs as well as enabling new features (e.g., concept-based overloading).

C++ template classes can be used to implement *type transformations.* Such a transformation take its input (the type to be transformed) as a template parameter, and the output is the instantiation of the template class with this parameter. Concepts can be used to ensure type conformance (both for the input and the output) and possibly drive some code specializations. However, they restrain the interface and the implementation of the newly created type: specific methods and associated types not mentioned in the concept of the input type will not be part of the new type. The paradigm of concept-based genericity lacks the required semantics to transform types while retaining or adapting their intrinsic capabilities.

This paper presents a new form of semantically-enriched genericity allowing static, generic type transformations through a simple form of type introspection based on type metadata called properties. This approach relies on a new Static C++ Object-Oriented Programming (SCOOP) paradigm [3], and is adapted to the creation of generic and efficient libraries, especially in the field of scientific computing [4, 5, 6, 7]. The exposed proposal uses a metaprogramming facility built into a C++ library called Static, and doesn't require any language extension nor additional processing (preprocessor or transformation tool).

# References

1. ISO/IEC: ISO/IEC 14882:2003 (e). Programming languages - C++ (2003)
2. Gregor, D., Järvi, J., Siek, J., Stroustrup, B., Reis, G.D., Lumsdaine, A.: Concepts: Linguistic support for generic programming in C++. In: Proceedings of the 2006 ACM SIGPLAN Conference on Object-Oriented Programming, Systems, Languages, and Applications (OOPSLA), pp. 291–310. ACM Press, New York (2006)
3. Burrus, N., Duret-Lutz, A., Geraud, T., Lesage, D., Poss, R.: A static C++ object-oriented programming (SCOOP) paradigm mixing benefits of traditional OOP and generic programming. In: Proceedings of the Workshop on Multiple Paradigm with Object-Oriented Languages (MPOOL), Anaheim, CA, USA (October 2003)
4. The Cgal Project: Cgal, Computational Geometry Algorithms Library (2008), http://www.cgal.org
5. Siek, J.G., Lee, L.Q., Lumsdaine, A.: The Boost Graph Library: User Guide and Reference Manual, 1st edn. C++ In-Depth Series. Addison Wesley Professional, Reading (2001)
6. Lombardy, S., Regis-Gianas, Y., Sakarovitch, J.: Introducing Vaucanson. Theoretical Computer Science 328, 77–96 (2004)
7. Duret-Lutz, A.: Olena: a component-based platform for image processing, mixing generic, generative and OO programming. In: Proceedings of the 2nd International Symposium on Generative and Component-Based Software Engineering (GCSE)-Young Researchers Workshop; published in Net.ObjectDays 2000, Erfurt, Germany, October 2000, pp. 653–659 (2000)

## 2.5    Functional Programming at Work in Object-Oriented Programming (with the C# Case) (Philippe Narbel)

This work presents a synthesis about why and how functional programming (FP) can be practically helpful within mainstream object-oriented programming (OOP). We first introduce criteria and rules to ensure that FP is actually effective within OOP. Next, we list and discuss the general techniques and design effects of having FP capabilities in OOP, including code abstraction/factoring at a function granularity level, generic iterator/loop implementations, operation compositions, sequence comprehensions, partial application and currying, limitations of the number of class definitions, name abstractions, and function-based structural compatibilities. We also stress some of the difficulties in blending FP and OOP by pointing out problems of *design granularity mismatch*, architecture non-uniformity and datatype incoherences. Several classic OOP design patterns are analyzed too, since FP techniques make alternative implementations possible: basic cases like Strategies, Commands and Observers, but also Proxies (using functional-based evaluation control) and Visitors (using functional data-driven programming). This synthesis is illustrated with C# 3.0 which offers effective FP-oriented features through so-called *delegates*, but also by using comparisons with other cross-paradigm languages.

Keywords: Object-oriented programming, functional programming, multi-paradigm programming, design patterns, closures, function objects, delegates, extension methods, open classes, C# 3.0, CLOS, Smalltalk, OCaml, Scala, Eiffel, Java 7.

# References

1. Beck, K.: Smalltalk Best Practice Patterns. Prentice-Hall, Englewood Cliffs (1997)
2. Gamma, E., Helm, R., Jonhnson, R., Vlissides, J.: Design Patterns. Addison-Wesley, Reading (1995)
3. Gabriel, R.P., White, J.L., Bobrow, D.G.: CLOS: integrating object-oriented and functional programming. Commun. ACM 34(9), 29–38 (1991)
4. Kühne, T.: A Functional Pattern System for Object-Oriented Design. Verlag Kovac (1999)
5. Meijer, E.: Confessions of a used programming language salesman. Getting the masses hooked on Haskell. In: OOPSLA 2007: Proceedings of the 22nd annual ACM SIGPLAN conference on Object oriented programming systems and applications, pp. 677–694 (2007)
6. McNamara, B., Smaragdakis, Y.: Functional programming with the FC++ library. J. Funct. Program. 14(4), 429–472 (2004)
7. Reynolds, J.C.: User-defined types and procedural data structures as complementary approaches to data abstraction. In: Schuman, A. (ed.) New Directions in Algorithmic Languages. IFIP Working Group 2.1 on Algol, pp. 157–168. INRIA (1975)
8. Wadler, P.: The expression problem. Java Genericity Mailing List (1998)

### 2.6    Object Based Multiparadigm Concepts for Verification of Functional Components (Máté Tejfel, Tamás Kozsik and Zoltán Horváth)

Temporal properties are very useful for proving the correctness of (sequential or parallel) object oriented programs. In the case of the correctness of components written in a functional programming language, the practicability of temporal operators is not so evident. In a pure functional language a variable is a value and not an object that can change its value in time, viz. during program execution. However, in some cases it is natural to express the knowledge about the computed values of the program in terms of temporal logical operators. Moreover, in the case of parallel, distributed and reactive functional programs or software composed both from object oriented and functional components temporal properties are also well applicable and necessary. The object abstraction technique can be used to identify expressions that the programmer considers the different states of the same abstract object, and to identify the state transitions. If an expression that is declared to be a state of a given abstract object depends on another expression that is also declared to be a state of that abstract object, the dependence is interpreted as a state transition. Temporal properties of abstract objects are expressed with respect to the state transitions.

An important class of software systems uses mobile components: components that are downloaded through the network and integrated into a running application. The correctness of these applications depends on the properties of the mobile components. In such cases the proof technique "composing specification" is applicable, which makes it possible to reason about the correctness of a compound system with respect to the properties of some of its components, even if these components themselves are unknown or the system is merged from functional, object oriented and other components. The Sparkle-T proof assistant provides tool support for managing composed specifications. The constructed proofs are represented in a machine processable form. As a consequence, not only the program but also its proved temporal properties and the proofs themselves can be stored, transmitted or checked by a computer. This allows the transmission of the code between two remote applications in a safe manner.

### 2.7    Implementation of JVM-Based Languages Support in IntelliJ IDEA (Ilya Sergey)

This work presents several examples of usage of two languages, compilable to Java byte-code, namely, Scala and Groovy. Author considers some functional and dynamic language constructs they bring to standard process of Java application development. For that purpose he appeals to the language analysis and IDE development process as comprehensive examples demonstrating the benefits of Scala and Groovy usage.

In fisrt part of present work author describes main stages of IDE development, such as lexical analysis, syntactic analysis and further semantic verifications. Some examples of replacing standard solutions in Java programming language by their functional analogues written on Scala are considered. Among other examples author describes LL(k) lexer implementaion using sequence comprehensions and implicit conversions, provided by Scala language. Unified approach to processing of files of different kinds, such as source files with program code, or compiled class-files, is also implemented using standard functional technics. Such Scala constructions as pattern matching, so-called case classes and extractors are used for that aim. Tree-like structures processing implementation in full measure uses power of higher order functions, such as foldLeft/Right, filter and map for standard Scala sequences. Another described design pattern is replacing of functions returning null value by others, which return instance of scala.Option[_] type.

Second part is concerned to Groovy programming language. Being dynamical language, Groovy provides rich opportunities for testing. Author describes implementation of well-known Builder design pattern via Groovy closures and mechanism of delegate substitution. Such approach allows to create mocked version of large objects, necessary for testing. Among other features "safe dereferencing" and "Groovy truth" concepts are considered as ways to decrease amount of boilerplate code. Last example is using of dynamic properties invocation for tuning in runtime some entities with big amount of settings. Both of considered languages were used in the process of language plugins development for IntelliJ IDEA. Source code of these projects is available for free download.

## 2.8   State-Oriented Programming (Asher Sterkin)

The traditional Object-Oriented approach, reflected in the State design pattern, suggests extracting complex state-dependant behavior into one or more separate objects and delegating to them decisions about which particular operations to perform. This solution, however, does not scale well for a large number of potential states/transitions. The same happens with developing an Object-Oriented solution for plain Final State Machines (FSMs): it is does not scale well for a large number of states and transitions unless the FSM is built automatically from some other formal description (e.g. regular expression).

Statecharts formalism suggests a scalable solution for state-dependent system modeling and specification. The Statechart formalism significantly reduces both the number of states and transitions by using hierarchical and parallel states, special event handlers, and shallow and deep history. Originally, Statecharts were associated with complex CAD tools such as iLogic Rhapsody or IBM/Rational Rose Real-Time. The main problem with these tools is a substantial mental gap between statechart diagrams and the code generated by the tool.

This paper introduces a new programming paradigm, called State-Oriented Programming, where statecharts are implemented as an internal Domain-Specific Language directly embedded into a mainstream Object-Oriented programming language such as Java, Groovy, Ruby, etc.

Embedding a Statechart Domain Specific Language (DSL) within a General Object-Oriented Programming Language (GOPL) turns out to be a complex mapping problem where various elements of the Statechart formalism (states, transitions, guards, actions) need to be mapped onto different elements of the hosting programming language (classes, methods, fields, templates, annotations and aspects).

This article presents a Generic Statechart Library (GSL), which provides a cost-effective implementation of an essential subset of Statechart formalism, suitable for user interface intensive and communication systems. Special attention is paid to code readability and trying to make GSL constructs look as close as possible to the hosting language.

Limitations of Java meta-programming capabilities are demonstrated. GSL implementation in Groovy is presented and advantages of dynamic Object-Oriented programming languages family (Groovy, Ruby) are discussed.

## 3    List of Participants

Oscar N. Nierstrasz
University of Berne, Switzerland
oscar@iam.unibe.ch

Asher Sterkin
NDS Israel
asterkin@nds.com

Ilya Sergey
SPBSU, Russia
ilya.sergey@jetbrains.com

Laurent Plagne
EDF R&D France
laurent.plagne@edf.fr

Zoltan Porkolab
Eötvös University, Budapest, Hungary
gsd@elte.hu

Zoltan Horvath
Eötvös University, Budapest, Hungary
hz@inf.elte.hu

Henrik Nilsson
University of Nottingham, UK
nhn@cs.nott.ac.uk

Thierry Geraud
EPITA R&D Lab, France
theo@lrde.epita.fr

Francesca Arcelli
University Milano-Bcocca, Italy
arcelli@disco.unimib.it

Paola Giannini
Università del Piemonte Orientale, Italy
giannini@mfn.unipmn.it

Markus Blatt
University Stuttgart, Germany
mblatt@gmx.net

Massimiliano Virdis,
Università di Cagliari
virdis@dsf.unica.it

Reza Ansari
University Paris Sud / LAL-Orsay, France
ansani@lal.in2p3.fr

Ramine Nikoukhah
INRIA, France
ramine.nikoukhah@inria.fr

David Pearce
Victoria University of Wellington, New Zealand
david.pearce@mcs.vuw.ac.nz

Stephen Nelson
Victoria University of Wellington, New Zealand
stephen@mcs.vuw.ac.nz

Peter Gottschling
TU Dresden, Germany
peter.gottschling@tu-dresden.de

## 4   The Organizers

**Jörg Striegnitz, Chair**, received his Diploma and Ph.D. in Computer Science from University of Technology at Aachen, Germany. He is now working as a professor for theoretical computer science and programming languages at the University Of Applied Sciences in Regensburg, Germany. His research work includes the integration of programming languages by means of partial evaluation, the application of multiparadigm programming to real world problems, the optimization of programs, and parallel/high performance scientific computing.

He authored the FACT! and the EML C++ libraries, that allow for functional programming style with C++.

Prof. Jörg Striegnitz
University Of Applied Sciences Regensburg
93053 Regensburg, Germany
joerg.striegnitz@informtik.fh-regensburg.de
http://homepages.fh-regensburg.de/~stj39817/people/striegnitz.html

**Kei Davis, Co-chair**, Ph.D. Computing Science (Glasgow), M.Sc. Computation (Oxford), is a research scientist at Los Alamos National Laboratory, U.S.A. He has conducted research in object-oriented and functional language technology for natural language processing, large system design and implementation, scripting, signal processing, parallel discrete-event simulation, and parallel/high performance scientific computing.

Dr. Kei Davis
Advanced Computing Laboratory, CCS-1
Los Alamos National Laboratory
Los Alamos, NM 87545, USA
kei.davis@lanl.gov
http://www.c3.lanl.gov/~kei

**Gerald Baumgartner** received a Diploma degree from the University of Linz, Austria, and M.S. and Ph.D. degrees from Purdue University, all in computer science. He is currently assistant professor in the Department of Computer Science at Louisiana State University. His research interest includes the design and implementation of object-oriented languages, search-based optimization algorithms, domain-specific languages and tools for high-performance computing, and testing tools for object-oriented programming and embedded systems programming. His extension of C++ with structural subtyping has been publicly available as part of the GNU C++ compiler, version 2.8. He is working on the design and implementation of Brew, an extension of Java with support for functional programming, multimethod dispatch, and retroactive abstraction.

Dr. Gerald Baumgartner Dept. of Computer Science
Louisiana State University
298 Coates Hall
Baton Rouge, LA 70803
Email: gb at csc.lsu.edu
http://www.csc.lsu.edu/~gb/

Zoltán Horváth OC Co-chair of ECOOP 2001, Member of AITO, Designer of programming language concepts connecting distributed functional programming with OO programming.

Prof. Zoltán Horváth, PhD, habil.
Department of Programming Languages and Compilers
Faculty of Informatics
University Eötvös Loránd of Sciences, Budapest, Hungary
hz@inf.elte.hu
http://people.inf.elte.hu/hz

Jaakko Järvi is an assistant professor in the Department of Computer Science at Texas A&M University. He has a Ph.D. in Computer Science from the University of Turku, Finland. His research interests include generic programming, programming languages, and software construction in general. He actively participates in the C++ standards committee and is a contributing member of the C++ Boost community, where his previous work has included template libraries that bring functional programming features to C++.

Dr. Jaakko Järvi
Department of Computer Science
Texas A&M University
College Station, TX 77843-3112, USA
Email: jarvi@cs.tamu.edu
http://faculty.cs.tamu.edu/jarvi

Herbert Kuchen received his Diploma, Ph.D., and Habilitation in computer science from the University of Technology at Aachen, Germany. He is now working as a professor for computer science at the University of Münster, Germany. He is interested in algorithmic skeletons for parallel programming and in the integration of programming paradigms, in particular in the combination of functional, logic, and object oriented programming, and he has been on many program committees of corresponding conferences. Recently, he developed a C++ skeleton library.

Prof. Herbert Kuchen
University of Münster
Leonardo Campus 3
48149 Münster, Germany
kuchen@uni-muenster.de

Erik Meijer is an architect in the Data Programmability Team in SQL Server where he works with the C# and Visual Basic teams on language and typesystems for data integration in programming languages. Prior to joining Microsoft he was an associate professor at Utrecht University and adjunct professor at the Oregon Graduate Institute. Erik is one of the designers of the Mondrian scripting language, standard functional programming language Haskell98, and Comega.

# Equation-Based Object-Oriented Languages and Tools

## Report on the 2nd Workshop EOOLT at ECOOP 2008

Peter Fritzson[1], David Broman[1], and François Cellier[2]

[1] Linköping University, Sweden
{davbr,petfr}@ida.liu.se
[2] ETH Zurich, Switzerland
fcellier@inf.ethz.ch

**Abstract.** EOOLT'2008 was the second edition of the ECOOP-EOOLT workshop. The workshop is intended to bring researchers associated with different equation-based object-oriented (EOO) modeling languages and different application areas making use of such languages together. The aim of the workshop is to explore common grounds and derive software design principles that may make future EOO modeling languages more robust, more versatile, and more widely accepted among the various stakeholders. At EOOLT'2008, researchers with diverse backgrounds and needs came together to present and discuss fourteen different concept papers grouped into the four topic areas of integrated system modeling approaches; modeling for multiple applications; modeling language design, and equation handling, diagnosis, and modeling.

## 1 Objectives and Call for Papers

Computer aided modeling and simulation of complex systems, using components from multiple application domains, such as electrical, mechanical, hydraulic, control, etc., have in recent years witnessed a significant growth of interest. In the last decade, novel equation-based object-oriented (EOO) modeling languages, (e.g., Modelica, gPROMS, and VHDL-AMS) based on acausal modeling using equations have appeared. Using such languages, it has become possible to model complex systems covering multiple application domains at a high level of abstraction through reusable model components.

The interest in EOO languages and tools is rapidly growing in the industry because of their increasing importance in modeling, simulation, and specification of complex systems. There exist several different EOO language communities today that grew out of different application areas (multi-body system dynamics, electronic circuit simulation, chemical process engineering). The members of these disparate communities rarely talk to each other in spite of the similarities of their modeling and simulation needs.

The workshop is concerned with, but not limited to, the following themes:

- Acausality and its role in model reusability.
- Component systems for EOO languages.
- Database lookup and knowledge invocation.
- Discrete-event and hybrid modeling using EOO languages.
- Embedded systems.

P. Eugster (Ed.): ECOOP 2008 Workshop Reader, LNCS 5475, pp. 18–29, 2009.
© Springer-Verlag Berlin Heidelberg 2009

- EOO language constructs in support of simulation, optimization, diagnostics, and system identification.
- EOO mathematical modeling vs. UML modeling.
- Equation-based languages supporting DAEs and/or PDEs.
- Formal semantics of EOO related languages.
- Multi-resolution / multi-scale modeling using EOO languages.
- Numerical coupling of EOO simulators and other simulation tools.
- Parallel execution of EOO models.
- Performance issues.
- Programming / modeling environments.
- Real-time simulation using EOO languages.
- Reflection and meta-programming.
- Reuse of models in EOO languages.
- Table lookup and interpolation.
- Type systems and early static checking.
- Verification.

The EOOLT workshop series aims at bringing these different communities together to discuss their common needs and goals as well as language semantics, algorithms, and tools that best support them.

The workshop is intended to become recurrent since this is an important and growing area of research and technology development.

The EOOLT Workshop addresses the current state of the art of EOO modeling languages as well as open issues that currently still limit the expression power and usefulness of such languages through a set of full-length presentations, short position papers, and forum discussions.

Papers and contributions are welcome that offer presentations and discussions of existing languages and tools, their capabilities and limitations; reports on practical experience; demonstrations of languages, tools, ideas, and concepts; positions related to relevant questions; and discussion topics.

Despite the fact that this is a not very established workshop series, there was a good response to the call-for-papers. Thirteen papers out of fifteen submissions were accepted to the workshop program. Additionally, there was an invited keynote presentation and associated extended abstract on Multi-Paradigm Language Engineering and Equation-Based Object-Oriented Languages. All papers were subject to at least three reviews by the program committee, some received four to five reviews.

The workshop program started with a welcome and introduction to the area of equation-based object-oriented languages, followed by paper presentations and discussion sessions after presentations of each set of related papers. EOOLT'2008 was held in Paphos, Cyprus, in conjunction with the ECOOP'2008 conference.

## 2  Organizers

**Peter A. Fritzson** received his M.Sc. in engineering 1975 and Ph.D. in computer science 1984, both from Linköping University. He is Professor and Director of the Programming Environment Laboratory (Pelab), at the Department of Computer and Information Science, Linköping University, Sweden. Peter Fritzson is vice chairman of the Modelica Association, an organization he helped to establish, and during 1999-2007 served as chairman of the Scandinavian Simulation Society, and secretary of the European simulation organization, EuroSim. His main area of interest is software engineering, especially languages, programming and debugging tools and environments; during recent years with special emphasis on modeling and simulation, and is currently leading the OpenModelica modeling and simulation open source tool effort. Professor Fritzson has authored or co-authored approximately 200 technical publications, including 14 books/proceedings. In 1994 he published a textbook "Principles of Object-Oriented Modeling and Simulation with Modelica", 939 pages, Wiley-IEEE Press. He has served as chair of a number of international conferences and workskops, and took the initiative to start the AADEBUG and EOOLT workshop series.

Prof. Dr.-Ing. Peter Fritzson
Programming Environment Laboratory (PELAB)
Linköping University
SE-581 83 Linköping
Sweden
Phone: +46(13)281484
Fax:    +46(13)285899
Mobile: +46(708)281484
Email:   petfr@ida.liu.se
URL:    http://www.ida.liu.se/labs/pelab/

**François E. Cellier** received his BS degree in electrical engineering in 1972, his MS degree in automatic control in 1973, and his PhD degree in technical sciences in 1979, all from the Swiss Federal Institute of Technology (ETH) Zurich. Dr. Cellier worked at the University of Arizona as professor of Electrical and Computer Engineering from 1984 until 2005. He recently returned to his home country of Switzerland where he assumed a position with ETH Zurich. Dr. Cellier's main scientific interests concern modeling and simulation methodologies, and the design of advanced software systems for simulation, computer aided modeling, and computer-aided design. Dr. Cellier has authored or co-authored more than 200 technical publications, and he has edited several books. He published a textbook on Continuous System Modeling in 1991 and a second textbook on Continuous System Simulation in 2006, both with Springer-Verlag, New York. He served as general chair or program chair of many international conferences, and served recently as president of the Society for Modeling and Simulation International.

Prof. Dr. François E. Cellier
Institute of Computational Science
CAB G82.1
ETH Zürich
CH-8092 Zürich
Switzerland
Phone: +41(44)632-7474
Fax:    +41(44)632-1374
Mobile: +41(79)416-7546
Email:   fcellier@inf.ethz.ch
URL:    http://www.inf.ethz.ch/~fcellier/

**David Broman** is currently pursuing his PhD in computer science at Linköping University, Sweden, where he also received his Licentiate degree in 2008 and M.Sc. degree in 2001. Before he started his PhD work, he worked as a software engineer and technical project manager for a security company in Stockholm. David's current research interest is focusing on language semantics and type systems of equation-based object-oriented languages. He is a member of the Modelica Association and has been active in the Modelica design group since 2005.

David Broman
Department of Computer and Information Science
Linköping University
SE-581 83 Linköping
Sweden
Phone: +46(0)13-285724
Fax: +46(0)13-285899
Mobile: +46(0)707-909075
URL: http://www.ida.liu.se/~davbr/

# 3  Participants

There were fourteen participants from eight different countries taking part of the second EOOLT workshop.

| Name | Affiliation | Country | Email |
|------|-------------|---------|-------|
| David Broman | Linköping University | Sweden | davbr@ida.liu.se |
| Francesco Casella | Politecnico di Milano | Italy | casella@elet.polimi.it |
| François E. Cellier | ETH Zurich | Switzerland | fcellier@inf.ethz.ch |
| Peter Fritzson | Linköping University | Sweden | petfr@ida.liu.se |
| Alberto Jorrín | University of Valladolid | Spain | albejor2002@hotmail.com |
| Malte Lochau | TU Braunschweig | Germany | lochau@ips.cs.tu-bs.de |
| Loucas Louca | University of Cyprus | Cyprus | lslouca@ucy.ac.cy |
| Masoud Najafi | Inria | France | masoud.najafi@inria.fr |
| Ramine Nikoukhah | Inria | France | ramine.nikoukhah@inria.fr |
| Henrik Nilsson | University of Nottingham | UK | nhn@cs.nott.ac.uk |
| Olaf Enge-Rosenblatt | Fraunhofer Institute for Integrated Circuits | Germany | olaf.enge@eas.iis.fraunhofer.de |
| Victorino Sanz | UNED, Madrid | Spain | vsanz @dia.uned.es |
| Hans Vangheluwe | McGill University | Canada | hv@cs.mcgill.ca |
| Dirk Zimmer | ETH Zurich | Switzerland | dzimmer@inf.ethz.ch |

# 4  Contributions

All papers are published electronically by Linköping University Electronic Press and available in the electronic proceedings at http://www.ep.liu.se/ecp/029/

All presentations (together with the papers) are also available at the EOOLT'2008 web site: http://www.eoolt.org/2008/

The workshop sessions are briefly described below. Each session started with paper presentations, followed by a discussion related to the topic of that particular session. Some discussion also took place during the paper presentations.

## 4.1  Integrated System Modeling Approaches

Session chair: François E. Cellier

This session grouped papers that especially emphasized integrated modeling tools for complex systems and integrated modeling environments aimed towards the whole development process.

In "Multi-Paradigm Language Engineering and Equation-Based Object-Oriented Languages," Hans Vangheluwe presented recent work on Multi-Paradigm Modeling (MPM). Whereas EOO languages make it a point to not hard-encode physical knowledge in their compilers, thereby providing the modeler with full flexibility in formulating models of different types of physical systems, they offer little in terms of helping the modeler structure the facets of physical knowledge that are to be encoded. MPM languages are located at a higher abstraction level. They support the modeler in formulating facets of physical knowledge, and offer meta-tools to transform these models algorithmically to a consistent framework, e.g. for use by an EOO environment.

In "Seamlessly Integrating Software & Hardware Modelling for Large-Scale System," Toby Myers, Peter Fritzson, and Geoff Dromey presented a method of integrating the software engineering approach, Behavior Engineering, with the mathematical modeling approach, Modelica, to address the software/hardware integration problem. The environment and hardware components are modeled in Modelica and integrated with an executable software model designed using Behavior Engineering. This allows the complete system to be simulated and interactions between software and hardware to be investigated early in development. A case study of the method was presented, including a model and simulation of an integrated BE and Modelica model of a train ATP system.

In "The Impreciseness of UML and Implications for ModelicaML," Jörn Guy Süß, Peter Fritzson, and Adrian Pop introduced ModelicaML as a meta-modeling environment for Whole Product Modeling. Modelica has been designed for mathematically representing physical systems (hardware), which it does very well. The language is not as powerful for dealing with mathematical descriptions of control actions (software) on these models, partly because of the sequential nature of these control actions, and partly because of the need to translate these control actions separately for downloading them into real-time controllers. Whereas UML is conceptually capable of representing all models, the full UML language definition is so powerful that no complete implementations exist at present. Furthermore, different subset implementations are incompatible with each other. The language specification is also ambiguous.

The paper proposed to limit the meta-modeling environment to a small subset of UML that can be well and unambiguously implemented in ModelicaML.

The subsequent discussion focused primarily on the first paper of the session. In particular, it was mentioned that ECOOP offers a separate workshop, MPOOL, on multi-paradigm languages. In spite of the obvious synergies between the two workshop topics, the EOOLT and MPOOL communities are currently almost entirely disjoint. It might be useful to establish a dialog at the level of the organizers of these two workshops to discuss how the synergies can be better exploited in the future.

In the context of meta-modeling, the question was raised how the correctness of large multi-faceted models can be ascertained, especially across the barrier between different modeling paradigms. Whereas a number of new tools were developed recently in the context of EOO languages for model validation and simulation verification purposes, there are no such tools available yet at the meta-modeling level. This issue requires further investigations.

Another issue that was raised concerns the formulation of adequate error messages following run-time exceptions. This issue is still problematic within the current generation of EOO languages, but will become even harder in the context of meta-modeling environments.

### 4.2  Modeling for Multiple Applications

Session chair: David Broman
The session concerned different applications and approaches of using models beyond the scope of simulation. Three papers were presented and discussed around the topic.

In "Multi-Aspect Modeling in Equation-Based Languages" Dirk Zimmer describes how models in EOO-languages typically include several other model aspects besides the physical model, such as system hints, 3D visualization, GUI-representation, and documentation. The need for and the current situation of handling these aspects are discussed with focus on the Modelica language. An alternative approach of separating these aspects is proposed, by introducing four new language constructs in the research language Sol. The need is also emphasized for a language to be able to extend itself concerning these aspects, without requiring the redefinition of the language specification.

In "Beyond Simulation: Computer Aided Control System Design Using Equation-Based Object-Oriented Modeling for the Next Decade" Francesco Casella, Filippo Donida, and Marco Lovera, discuss the need for EOO-languages and tools to support and focus on other usages than simulation. An overview of state-of-the-art of designing advanced model-based control-systems based on EOO-models is given. This is followed by a number of proposals for future development in the area, e.g., open model exchange formats, automated model order reduction, automatic derivation of linear fractional transformations (LFT) models, inverse models for robotic system, and support for nonlinear model predictive control (MPC).

In "A Static Aspect Language for Modelica Models" Malte Lochau and Henning Günther present a declarative language for specifying and evaluating quantified rules for static properties of Modelica models. The language makes use of aspect oriented programming (AOP) and the proposed framework is based on logic meta-programming, where Prolog can serve as evaluation engine. Examples of application areas were given and the balanced model requirement of Modelica 3.0 was proposed as a case study for future work.

In the following discussion session, several questions were raised. One concern discussed regarding control system applications, such as model reduction and optimization, was the extensive computational requirements. Another issue discussed and agreed upon was the need of keeping the models for control application physical.

Another topic discussed concerning other model aspects than physical properties of Modelica models, was the use of annotations. The problem of vendor specific annotations was highlighted as a major portability issue. It was further discussed how interfaces and specific built in language constructs could help in the situation of portability. If interfaces are defined, but the semantics are left to the tool vendor, does not this give the same problem as with annotations? It was concluded that this was probably inevitable.

A question was raised regarding how name bindings were handled in the static aspect oriented language given in presentation 3. It was concluded that this is a very complex problem and regarded as future work.

To summarize, both the presentations and the following discussion showed a clear need for further research in the area of other usages of EOO models than simulation.

### 4.3  Modeling Language Design

Session chair: Peter Fritzson
This session concerned papers on the topic of modeling language design, including new language constructs, novel type systems and type analysis, and a description of an existing language.

In "Higher-Order Acausal Models", David Broman and Peter Fritzson presents the idea of higher-order acausal models (HOAM), inspired by the concept of higher-order functions in functional programming, but extended to acausal models. HOAM allows models to take models as input, and generate models as results. This allows model transformations including general model composition and recursion operations and does not require data representation/reification of models as in traditional metaprogramming/metamodeling. Examples of using HOAMs within the electrical and mechanical domain are also presented.

In "Type-Based Structural Analysis for Modular Systems of Equations", Henrik Nilsson investigates a novel approach to a type system for modular systems of equations, i.e., composition of equation systems from acausal model fragments/modules containing equations. Attributing a structural type to equation system fragments allows aspects of insolvability such as over- and underdetermined system fragments to be identified, without first having to assemble these into a full system of equations. The main issue is handling abstraction of systems of equations, for which the paper presents an algorithm for determining the best possible type. This is still work in progress, and the presented type system is not yet complete.

In "Introducing Messages in Modelica for Facilitating Discrete-Event System Modeling", Victorino Sanz, Alfonso Urquía, and Sebastián Dormido presents a language extension to Modelica, with messages and mailboxes, to facilitate process-oriented modeling of discrete-event based applications. The author's found this to be a difficult using current Modelica, which they have implemented in the libraries

ARENALib, SIMANLib, and DEVSLib. These libraries still have some problems without a solution, like one-to-many connections in DEVSLib and polymorphism of information transmitted at event instants. The proposed language extension should handle these problems and facilitate discrete-event process-oriented modeling. A possible implementation for Modelica is also presented.

In "EcosimPro and its EL Object-Oriented Modeling Language" Alberto Jorrín, César de Prada, and Pedro Cobas presents the EcosimPro modeling and simulation environment with the EL (EcosimPro Language) acausal modeling language. The presentation covers acausal object-oriented language features such as classes, components, connections, inheritance, etc., very similar to an EOO language such as Modelica, as well as the concept of experiment.

Regarding the first talk, one comment was that we need to be clear about the concept of higher-order. Higher-order in traditional mathematical modeling means higher order derivates, whereas in this paper and in functional programming higher-order means the property of objects (or in HOAMs, models) being first-class entities in the language, i.e., passed to models, returned from models, etc. Another question concerned debugging of higher order models, will it be more complicated to detect an error and correct it in a higher-order language than in a conventional language. To summarize, the HOAM approach was considered general and powerful.

Regarding the second presentation, on type-based structural analysis, there were questions about language restrictions to support better checking (as currently in the Modelica design effort). Can this idea about type-based structural analysis be applied to Modelica by enhancing the Modelica type system? Answer: this might be possible, but would need additional work. For example, handling constructions such as inner/outer. A general comment: both this approach and the constraint delta approach are conservative approaches, using a type system to perform partial checking of equation system solvability.

The third talk was about new message primitives in Modelica, for better supporting discrete-event process modeling. One question concerned declarativeness, will not these extensions destroy the declarative properties of Modelica, since you rely on the order of events and messages? The answer was that in process modeling, you want to model such properties explicitly. However, there is of course the danger of misuse of such language primitives. Another comment: if you are not careful, you will just re-implement ARENA. Also, you have to be careful if you mix this with continuous-time modeling. A follow-up comment: a different direction might be to change things and translate into DEVS instead of using Modelica when? However, still symbolic optimization would be needed. There is also the issue of performance. Another direction would be to come up with a declarative specification of a discrete-event system, e.g. a logical formulation of discrete events? Another question: would it be meaningful to solve event systems backwards? To specify outputs and solve for inputs? An answer: diagnostic people do this, which leads to trees, i.e., not a unique solution. This might make the situation worse.

The fourth talk was about the EcosimPro environment ant the EL language. A general question: what is the difference compared to Modelica? The languages are rather similar. No clear answer was given. Another question: Is EL really the official European Space Agency (ESA) language, since it is known that some parts of ESA are using Modelica?

## 4.4   Equation Handling, Diagnosis, and Modeling

Session chair: François E. Cellier

This session presented four papers discussion different aspects of EOO languages and tools.

In "Activation Inheritance in Modelica," Ramine Nikoukhah presented an ambiguity in the Modelica language concerning the handling of concurrent events. Some events are concurrent, because they happen at the same time, although they are not logically connected with each other; others occur simultaneously, because they are logically related. The modeling language should offer means to distinguish between these two types of synchronicity, and offered a proposed syntax that can take care of the problem.

In "Selection of Variables in Initialization of Modelica Models," Masoud Najafi presented a GUI for initialization of variables as implemented in Scicos. Modelica offers different ways of specifying initial conditions, but doesn't offer much in terms of support for helping the user specify a complete and linearly independent set of initial conditions. The GUI presented in this paper takes care of this problem.

The third paper of the session: "Supporting Model-Based Diagnostics with Equation-Based Object Oriented Languages," by Peter Bunus and Karin Lunde was not presented as neither of the two authors participated in the conference.

In "Towards an Object-oriented Implementation of von Mises' Motor Calculus Using Modelica," Tobias Zaiczek and Olaf Enge-Rosenblatt presented an alternative approach to the method embraced in the Modelica Standard Library (MSL) for mathematically describing multi-body systems (MBS). In MBS dynamics, the modeler has a choice of what state variables to use. The selection of the set of state variables influences strongly both the efficiency of the generated simulation code and the error propagation during simulation. The MSL embraces the theory of order-n models, whereas this paper advocates the use of another approach by Mises, an approach that has been known for many years, but hadn't been implemented in Modelica.

In the following discussion, regarding talk 1, Dirk Zimmer remarked that the handling of synchronous simultaneous events doesn't work correctly in Dymola as of now. The event detection algorithm, as currently implemented in Dymola, depends on the passing of time, and when zero time passes between one event and the next, the second event is not detected. Ramine Nikoukhah also remarked that the semantics of algorithmic sections outside of when clauses are not clearly defined. It matters in which order they are being executed, yet the modeler has no control over this issue.

Regarding the second talk, François Cellier noticed that the GUI, as currently implemented in Scicos, defeats the concept of object orientation. Francesco Casella remarked that the initialization problem is always global. We don't have a good approach yet to object-oriented initialization. François Cellier also observed that initialization happens not only at the beginning of the simulation, but after each event. The GUI only looks at the original initialization problem.

Finally, regarding the third talk (fourth paper), François Cellier asked whether the authors had already looked at the number of simulation equations generated when using the Mises approach. The approach could only be competitive if the number of simulation equations grows linearly with the number of bodies. Olaf Enge-Rosenblatt answered that they hadn't looked at this issue yet, but would do so in the future.

# 5  Discussion of Future Directions of EOOLT

The workshop ended with a general discussion about possible future directions of EOO languages and tools, and the EOOLT workshop itself. The discussion was roughly divided into the following three areas.

## 5.1  Which Are the Most Important Current Problems in EOOLT?

This is the list of the most important EOOLT current problems mentioned during the discussion (in no particular order):

- Events in EOO, how to integrate EOO and events, e.g. DEVS, Synchronization, etc.
- Functional approach, more functional programming ideas transferred into EOO, also ideas from OO + functional integration.
- Systems engineering, integrating software and hardware modeling.
- Mapping execution back to source model, needed for traceability and debugging.
- Better tool interoperability and modularity (c.f. the Unix processes and pipe example).
- More precise semantics, definitions, also including definition through meta-programming/meta-modeling. Development of a canonical flattening form with test suite.
- Applications of EOO not only for simulation, e.g. optimization, controllers, etc. Meta-modeling and tools, also including scripting, for modular solutions.

## 5.2  Main Motivation for the Creation of the EOOLT Workshop Series

The participants reviewed the main motivations for the EOOLT workshop series, which were still considered relevant:

- Be a common forum for several communities in Equation-Based Object-Oriented Languages and Tools.
- Get more involvement and interest from computer scientists in EOO research.

## 5.3  Which Conference for the EOOLT Workshop to Associate with?

One of the main motivations for EOOLT is to try to get more joint interest with computer science. Which is the best conference to be associated with?

Continue with ECOOP?

- Pros: Already ongoing co-location. ECOOP is a well-known language conference, covering areas such as OO programming, type systems, OO parallelism.
- Cons: ECOOP people are not interested in modeling, they are mostly interested in Java- or Smalltalk-like OO programming. The conference time is also a bit inconvenient, during (Swedish/US/etc.) vacation time in July.

The model-driven conference ECMDA-FA (prev. MDAFA)
(www.fokus.fraunhofer.de/go/ecmda2008/)

- Pros: Model-driven development. Also industrial and Eclipse. Has workshops. In Europe.
- Cons: Perhaps too much focus on the modeling environment Eclipse, compared to modeling and modeling language issues.

Modeling conference MODELS (www.models.org)

- Pros: Well established software modeling conference. Tracks state-of-the-art. Multi-paradigm modeling workshop has been successful. Meta-modeling, SysML, model transformations.
- Cons: Too much UML? There might already be too many workshops at MODELS?

Systems Engineering Conference: INCOSE or SEA

- Pros: EOO is very important for systems engineering.
- Cons: Perhaps too few computer scientists? Perhaps too narrow focus?

## 6  Conclusions

The participants felt that this second EOOLT also was a successful workshop. The area of equation-based object-oriented (EOO) languages and tools is of rapidly increasing importance. It is still important to engage more computer scientists in this area, which is one of the motivations of co-locating the workshop with ECOOP.

On the other hand, even though ECOOP and EOOLT have the topic of object orientation in common, it was felt that there is too little overlap between EOOLT and ECOOP. The usual ECOOP attendees seem to be primarily interested in object-oriented programming, but not in modeling, even if it is object-oriented. Many ECOOP people don't even know about modeling. It was discussed whether to move the workshop to be held in conjunction with another conference where people have more interest in modeling. Candidates such as MODEL, ECMDA-FA, or system engineering conferences were mentioned.

To conclude, it was felt that the papers and workshop discussions were good, and that the workshop series should be continued. Some references are given below as a background to this area.

## References

[1] Accellera, Cadence: Verilog-AMS Language Reference Manual Version 2.2, Published by: Accellera, 1370 Trancas Street, #163, Napa, CA 94558 (November 2004)

[2] Augustin, D.C., Fineberg, M.S., Johnson, B.B., Linebarger, R.N., Sansom, F.J., Strauss, J.C.: The SCi Continuous System Simulation Language (CSSL). Simulation 9, 281–303 (1967)

[3] Birtwistle, G.M., Dahl, O.J., Myhrhaug, B., Nygaard, K.: SIMULA BEGIN. Auerbach Publishers, Inc. (1973)

[4] Breunese, A.P.J., Broenink, J.F.: Modeling Mechatronic Systems Using the SIDOPS+ Language. In: Proceedings of ICBGM 1997, 3rd International Conference on Bond Graph Modeling and Simulation, Phoenix, Arizona, vol. 29(1), pp. 301–306. SCS Publishing, San Diego (1997), http://www.rt.el.utwente.nl/proj/modsim/modsim.htm (January 12-15, 1997)

[5] Cellier, F.E.: Continuous System Modelling, 755 p. Springer, New York (1991)

[6] Cellier, F.E., Kofman, E.: Continuous System Simulation, 643 p. Springer, New York (2006)

[7] Christen, E., Bakalar, K.: VHDL-AMS – A Hardware Description Language for Analog and Mixed-Signal Applications. IEEE Transactions on Circuits and Systems II: Analog and Digital Signal Processing 46(10), 1263–1272 (1999)

[8] Clabaugh, J., Tolsma, J.E., Barton, P.I.: Abacuss II: Advanced Modeling Environment and Embedded Simulator, and Abacuss II Syntax Manual, Massachusetts Institute of Technology, Chemical Engineering System Research Group (1999), http://yoric.mit.edu/abacuss2/abacuss2.html

[9] Elmqvist, H.: A Structured Model Language for Large Continuous Systems. Ph.D. thesis, TFRT-1015, Department of Automatic Control, Lund Institute of Technology, Lund, Sweden (1978)

[10] Ernst, T., Jähnichen, S., Klose, M.: The Architecture of the Smile/M Simulation Environment. In: Proceedings 15th IMACS World Congress on Scientific Computation, Modelling and Applied Mathematics, Berlin, Germany, vol. 6, pp. 653–658 (1997)

[11] Fritzson, P.: Principles of Object-Oriented Modeling and Simulation with Modelica 2.1, 940 p. Wiley-IEEE Press, Chichester (2004)

[12] Fritzson, P., Viklund, L., Fritzson, D., Herber, J.: High Level Mathematical Modeling and Programming in Scientific Computing. IEEE Software, 77–87 (1995)

[13] Mattsson, S.-E., Andersson, M.: The Ideas Behind Omola. In: Proceedings of the 1992 IEEE Symposium on Computer-Aided Control System Design (CADCS 1992), Napa, California, March 17-19, pp. 23–29 (1992)

[14] Oh, M., Pantelides, C.C.: A modelling and Simulation Language for Combined Lumped and Distributed Parameter Systems. Computers and Chemical Engineering 20(6–7), 611–633 (1996)

[15] Piela, P.C., Epperly, T.G., Westerberg, K.M., Westerberg, A.W.: ASCEND: An Object-Oriented Computer Environment for Modeling and Analysis: The Modeling Language. Computers and Chemical Engineering 15(1), 53–72 (1991)

[16] Sahlin, P., Sowell, E.F.: A Neutral Format for Building Simulation Models. In: Proceedings of the Conference on Building Simulation, IBPSA, Vancouver, Canada, pp. 147–154 (1989)

[17] Sargent, R.W.H., Westerberg, A.W.: Speed-Up in Chemical Engineering Design. Chemical Engineering Research and Design 42a, 190–197 (1964)

[18] The Mathworks. Simulink – Simulation and Model-Based Design., http://www.mathworks.com/products/simulink/ (last accessed: 6 March 2007)

[19] The Modelica Association. The Modelica Language Specification Version 3.0 (September 2007), http://www.modelica.org

[20] Tiller, M.: Introduction to Physical Modeling with Modelica, 368 p. Springer, New York (2001)

[21] UML Homepage, http://www.uml.org

[22] van Beek, D.A., Man, K.L., Reniers, M., Rooda, J.E., Schiffelers, R.R.H.: Syntax, and consistent equation semantics of hybrid Chi. The Journal of Logic and Algebraic Programming 68, 129–210 (2006)

# Aliasing, Confinement, and Ownership in Object-Oriented Programming

## Report on the Workshop IWACO'08 at ECOOP 2008

Dave Clarke[1], Sophia Drossopoulou[2], Peter Müller[3], James Noble[4], and Tobias Wrigstad[5]

[1] Katholieke Universiteit Leuven, Belgium
Dave.Clarke@cs.kuleuven.be
[2] Imperial College, London, UK
sd@doc.ic.ac.uk
[3] ETH Zurich, Switzerland
peter.mueller@inf.ethz.ch
[4] Victoria University of Wellington, New Zealand
kjx@mcs.vuw.ac.uk
[5] Purdue University, USA
wrigstad@cs.purdue.edu

**Abstract.** The power of objects lies in the flexibility of their interconnection structure. But this flexibility comes at a cost. Because an object can be modified via any alias, object-oriented programs are hard to understand, maintain, and analyze. Aliasing makes objects depend on their environment in unpredictable ways, breaking the encapsulation necessary for reliable software components, making it difficult to reason about and optimize programs, obscuring the flow of information between objects, and introducing security problems.

Aliasing is a fundamental difficulty, but we accept its presence. Instead we seek techniques for describing, reasoning about, restricting, analyzing, and preventing the connections between objects and/or the flow of information between them. Promising approaches to these problems are based on ownership, confinement, information flow, sharing control, escape analysis, argument independence, read-only references, effects systems, and access control mechanisms.

## 1 Introduction

The aim of the IWACO workshop was to address the question how to manage interconnected object structures in the presence of aliasing. In, particular the following issues were covered:

- models, type and other formal systems, programming language, separation logic, mechanisms, analysis and design techniques, patterns, tools and notations for expressing object ownership, aliasing, confinement, uniqueness, and/or information flow;

P. Eugster (Ed.): ECOOP 2008 Workshop Reader, LNCS 5475, pp. 30–41, 2009.

- optimization techniques, analysis algorithms, libraries, applications, tools, and novel approaches exploiting object ownership, aliasing, confinement, uniqueness, and/or information flow;
- empirical studies of programs or experience reports from programming systems designed with these issues in mind;
- novel applications of aliasing management techniques such as ownership types, ownership domains, confined types, region types, and uniqueness.

**History.** IWACO 2008 was the fourth ECOOP workshop focusing on aliasing. The previous workshops were IWACO 2007 [11], IWACO 2003 [10], and the Intercontinental Workshop on Aliasing in Object-Oriented Systems (IWAOOS) in 1999. The issues addressed in this workshop were first brought into focus with the Geneva Convention on the Treatment of Object Aliasing [19].

**Program.** The workshop provided a forum for two invited talks, seven presentations of submitted papers (including three position papers), four tool demos, and ample discussions. It was organized in four sessions, which we summarize in the following four sections.

## 2   Session 1: Invited Talk

The presentation of our first invited speaker, Jonathan Aldrich from Carnegie Mellon University, was entitled "Define, don't Confine". It identified three major challenges that need to be addressed in order to bring alias control into practice.

First, the community has to identify *applications* where the benefit of making program structure explicit has a significant and immediate benefit. Two promising candidates are concurrency and verification. For both applications, it will be necessary to make the annotations lightweight (possibly through inference) and to improve the expressiveness in order to cover common program styles and idioms.

Second, the community has to increase the *adoptability* of alias control by reducing the annotation burden through inference and by providing support for existing languages and programs.

Third, the community has to increase the *applicability* of alias control to be able to handle more programs. Aldrich's position here is that the community has focused too much on *restricting* aliasing rather than *documenting* the aliasing in programs and using this information for reasoning. He showed various examples that support his position.

To the great satisfaction of the IWACO crowd, Aldrich's final slide was entitled "The Future of Alias Control is Bright"—provided that the three challenges will be addressed successfully.

## 3   Session 2: Ownership

Two of the open challenges for type systems expressing ownership and related properties are (1) determining *what* the type system should express and *how* it should express it, and (2) type inference. The four talks in the second session addressed one or both of these issues.

*Expressiveness.* A lot of research has gone into determining *how* to best express information such as ownership and immutability. As suggested in Aldrich's keynote, there needs to be shift more towards addressing *what* needs to be expressed, as directly extending existing type systems tends to intermingle the policy with the mechanism of the type system. Nonetheless, work on improving the expressiveness of individual type systems still produces useful technical machinery.

Yu David Liu presented *Pedigree Types*, joint work with Scott Smith. Pedigree types aim to obtain the benefits of owner parameterization, as in in Ownership Types [13], with the simple syntactic convenience of Universe Types [15].

Parameters are never explicitly stated on classes, and instead type inference is used to fill in types and class parameters omitted by the programmer. Ownership is described by adapting metaphors from human genealogy, which could aid programmers in understanding and expressing the ownership structure in their programs. Owners take the general form **parent**$^a$**.child**$^b$, describing a traversal up the ownership tree, and then down again, under the constraints that $a \geq 0$ and $b \in \{0, 1\}$. Existing owners can be described in a natural manner **rep** = **child**, **self** = **parent**$^0$**.child**$^0$, **sibling** = **peer** = **owner** = **parent.child**, along with new ones, such as **parent**, **grandparent** = **parent**$^2$, and **uncle** = **parent**$^2$**.child**$^1$. In principle, the types can also express owners not available and expressible in the other systems, such as whenever the child's index is greater than 1 an encapsulation violation occurs. Classes are (implicitly) parameterized by such indices, allowing classes to be used in different places with different pedigrees within an ownership tree. A natural notion of pedigree subsumption also exists, permitting the relationship **self** $\leq$ **sibling**, **parent** $\leq$ **uncle** = **parent**$^2$**.child**$^1$, and, more generally, **parent**$^a$**.child**$^b$ $\leq$ **parent**$^{a+1}$**.child**$^{b+1}$. The type system presented in the paper is sound and decidable. It can express deep ownership and has a natural runtime representation. Various extensions to the system are also described in the paper, including *opting-out*.

Alex Potanin presented the position paper *Towards Unifying Immutability and Ownership*, describing joint work with Paley Li, James Noble, and Lindsay Groves. The paper called for the unification of immutability and ownership in order to improve the expressiveness of each notion. The goal is not to merely put the two notions together in the same language, but to really unify them. The paper emphasized the need to avoid *observational exposure* [6], which requires that mutations to an object are not observed by other objects—this is essentially the difference between immutability and read-only. The paper presented three possible ways of unifying the two mechanisms, leveraging the Generic Ownership approach [29]. The three approaches were:

- direct combination of generic ownership and generic immutability—have separate parameter spaces representing ownership information and immutability information;

- generic immutability and ownership—combine the 'type' hierarchies representing ownership and immutability into one, thereby requiring only a single
parameter space to represent them; and
- generic access rights for immutability and ownership—define, more or less,
a language of access rights, along the lines of *Capabilities for Sharing* [7].

Some debate arose suggesting that a fourth possibility, namely, annotating the
owners with write/read-only/immutable access modes, as in $Joe_3$ [26], though
this needed external uniqueness [12] to work.

Nick Cameron presented the position paper *Variant Ownership with Existential Types*, joint work with Sophia Drossopoulou. The presentation described
various advantages and possibilities offered by existential types. The type system,
called $Jo\exists$, outlined ideas from Java's wildcards in the context of Generic Ownership, to gain expressiveness yet remain compatible with Java. Java's wildcards
soften the subtyping relation by allowing variance in a generic type's parameters. The main research issue with this work is whether adding existential types
opens the door too far. That is, if existential types are used to forget ownership
information, will the constraints imposed by ownership and the benefits thereby
gained be lost? It was conjectured that type (ownership) bounds could be used
to retain the information required to enforce such constraints, though further
research is required to determine whether this is the case. An additional open
question is that of decidability of the type system.

*Type Inference.* Developing type inference systems for type systems expressing
ownership is crucial for their adoption, as they are required to add annotations
to library code and to reduce the volume of annotations in programmers' code.
Two papers described various aspects of the inference process.

Yu David Liu's work reduces type inference to the problem of finding suitable
parent and child indices; thus, type inference can be expressed as a constraint
problem over integers. With previous attempts at type inference in parameterized
ownership type systems, the number of parameters can grow in an unbounded
manner. This was handled by unifying different possible parameters whenever a
recursive occurrence of a class was encountered.

Ana Milanova's presentation of *Static Inference of Universe Types* described
an algorithm for inferring Universe Types for Java programs. This work extends
her past research on inferring Ownership Types for Java programs [23]. The algorithm was based on a points-to analysis and performed the following steps:
construct static object graph; compute dominance boundary of each object; assign types to object graph edges; and assign types to fields and variables. The
approach aims to produce a deep tree, but whenever a write upwards in the tree
occurs, it forces a shallower ownership structure. The main challenge was that
there were many possible type assignments, and no precise notion of principal
assignment. Promising preliminary results were given.

An interesting open question is whether the two approaches can be combined.
That is, can the constraint-based approach be applied to Universe Types?

# 4  Session 3: Concurrency and Ownership Demos

*Concurrency.* Nicholas Matsakis presented joint work with Thomas Gross. They describe a flow sensitive type and effects system that requires methods to declare the partitions of the heap that are read or written, resp. Effect agreements can be used to limit the conditions in which a method can be called. With this system, multi-threaded programs follow safe conventions that guarantee the program is free of data races.

A partition is a compile-time abstraction that identifies a distinct set of locations (object-field pairs) in the heap. Partitions are similar to data groups [21], but have scope, which can be exploited to achieve, for example, thread-local state. Methods are annotated with five kinds of effects that they have on partitions: read, write, atomic read, atomic write, and intersection. Atomic read/write indicates that the partition was accessed from within a block guaranteed to execute atomically. An intersection effect records that two partitions were made to intersect: this needs to be made explicit and trackable by analysis because when two partitions intersect, data that is added to one must also be considered added to the other.

In addition to being annotated with effects, a method may also be annotated with a contract, known as an effect agreement, that constrains what can happen before the method is called or after it returns. Effect agreements are always in the negative, they describe what must not have occurred prior to invocation (pre agreements), and what must not happen after the method has returned (par agreements). A pre agreement is generally used to require that certain partitions have not been intersected and are thus known to be disjoint. A par agreement is used to indicate that the method has started a new thread and that certain effects should not happen in parallel with that thread's execution.

The discussion of this presentation focused on the relation with Dave Cunningham's work (to be presented at FTfJP the next day) as well as on some possible variants of the proposed annotations, as e.g., in Java wildcards.

John Boyland argued that Java's volatile fields are difficult to reason about in a strictly linear fashion as found in concurrent separation logic [8] or fractional permissions [5]. In these approaches, accesses to volatile fields can be modeled using atomic blocks and auxiliary state, which Boyland finds unsatisfying because such a description is rather low-level. Instead, volatile fields are more easily handled by using non-linear concepts such as immutability and ownership [9], where they can be treated as loop holes, that is, accesses to volatile fields are not checked by the system. Boyland argued that a combination of linear and non-linear reasoning is highly desirable. He encourages research in how to formalize ownership as a nonlinear subsystem in a mostly linear logic.

*Ownership Demos.* In the demo section of this session, Alex Potanin demonstrated the type checkers for Ownership Generic Java (OGJ) [29] and Immutable Generic Java (IGJ) [31]. Both systems build on Java generics to check the additional properties. Peter Müller presented some of the ETH tools for Universe Types, namely the type checkers for Generic Universe Types (GUT) [14] and

Universe Types with Transfer (UTT) [24]. Both Universe checkers are implemented in the compiler for the Java Modeling Language (JML) [20].

## 5  Session 4: Verification

The final session began with a second invited talk from Dino Distefano, describing his jStar system, based on a paper (with Matthew Parkinson) that he will present at OOPSLA later this year [17]. jStar's key contribution is that it is based on separation logic [28], rather than ownership, applying techniques from earlier separation logic based checkers [2,16] to object-oriented programs.

Being based on separation logic from the outset gives jStar a number of immediate advantages over ownership-based approaches such as JML [20] and Spec♯ [22]. First, jStar does not impose any restrictions on the topology or use of pointers in object-oriented programs: no "owners as dominators", "owners as modifiers", or "owners cover invariants" discipline is required in program design. Second, because of this lack of an ownership discipline, programmers do not have to annotate their programs to describe how particular classes use that disciple. Third, the only annotations (method pre- and post- conditions) that are required are much briefer than in ownership based systems, because a single annotation language (separation logic) covers both the propositional content of assertions and the framing required to deal with heap storage and delineate potential aliasing. Fourth, using only stand-alone predicates and eschewing class invariants means that many of the complexities of whether and when a class is in a "valid state" can be replaced by instantaneously asserting particular predicates [27]. On the other hand, of course, these advantages come at cost: principally, that programmers must write assertions in separation logics, rather than traditional computation logics.

The other advance embodied in jStar is the use of abductive reasoning for abstract reasoning, particularly, it seems, regarding heap topologies. jStar includes a set of inference rules that embody abstraction functions, taking lower level heap states (e.g., sequences of cons nodes) up to more abstract data structure (e.g., a list spine and its contents). This means that—compared with other systems, in some sense jStar performs something similar to "ownership inference" as well as program proving based on the inferred heap properties. This inference is not general purpose (as inference must for an ownership type system) but context specific: different sets of abstraction rules are required for significantly different implementations of each abstraction. For example, one rule set it seems can handle all kinds of singly-linked lists, but a doubly-linked list, or an array-list would require a different set of rules. The ability to customize jStar to handle different abstractions is clearly very powerful, and enables jStar to verify programs without any annotations other than pre and post conditions. These abstraction rules may turn out to be brittle in practice, or to need customizing to suit each system being verified—more experimentation is clearly needed here, but the demonstrated system was very promising!

At least for small examples, however, jStar provides a convincing argument for the benefits of this approach. jStar provides "full automatic" verification of a range of programs, even when incorporating examples that ownership-based systems find very difficult to model, such as the Observer pattern, structure sharing, and ownership transfer. As demonstrated, the performance of jStar doing full verification did not seem much slower than a Java compiler running on the same examples: raising the question of why bother with complex "intermediate" systems such as ownership (or even language-level types) if a program prover can verify programs without these annotations? On the other hand, it seems as if ownership systems can avoid the need for these inference rules, because programs' abstractions are already structured via ownership.

The second presentation in this session, by Christian Haack and Clément Hurlin, also used separation logic. Christian and Clément presented a series of specifications for Iterators of various different kinds. This separation logic uses a form of linear implication to represent state transitions (as well as heap separation) and includes Boyland-style fractional permissions [18]. These features enable the system easily to encompass typestate-style modeling (e.g., an iterator is ready for reading; has been accessed; or is at the end of the traversal) and to distinguish between read-write, read-only, and immutable accesses to objects.

The key contribution of this work seems to be that the Iterator specifications are parameterized. The final declaration of an Iterator interface is:

```
interface Iterator
/*@<perm p, boolean isdeep, Collection<isdeep> iteratee>@*/
```

with three parameters p, isdeep, and iteratee. (In this system, specifications are given in extended comment syntax.) The iteratee parameter is the most straightforward to explain; it is the collection to be iterated over. The p parameter is a fractional permission (thus perm) controlling access to the collection: set to 1, the Iterator has exclusive (and thus read-write) access to the collection, set to less than one, the Iterator has shared (read-only) access to the collection. Finally the third parameter isdeep captures an ownership relation between the container and its elements: a "deep" collection owns its elements while a "shallow" collection does not. (Note that distinction is similar to that between "full" and "flexible" alias protection [25], although the alias protection schemes controlled references, while the these separation-based schemes control only the permission to read or write references.) Then, a single specification for an iterator protocol can be configured in a number of different ways: an iterator over a collection of immutable elements; as a set of concurrent read-only iterators; or a shallow iterator over a mutable collection.

This presentation again demonstrated the utility of separation logic for describing complex and flexible structures, especially where structure sharing is involved, and the parameterization mechanism clearly makes specifications more concise, especially where families of related specifications are concerned. A particularly interesting feature of this work was the "isdeep" ownership parameter: it is not clear whether this is an accident of the particular specification examples chosen, or illustrates some more essential role for ownership even in systems where the underlying representation is separation logic.

The workshop was bookended with a tool demo by Jonathan Aldrich, who also opened the workshop. He demonstrated the Plural tool, work carried out with his student Kevin Bierhoff [4]. Plural is a practical typestate checker for object-oriented programs, a successor to Rob DeLine and Manuel Fähndrich's Fugue [30] in that both systems model abstractions of objects' state and check that methods are only called on objects in permissible states. The key difference between Plural and Fugue is that Plural's analyses are based on permissions (similar to Boyland's capabilities for sharing [7] and fractional permissions [5]). In contrast to Fugue, where an object could only change typestate while it was unique, Plural's permissions mean that typestate analysis is feasible in the presence of aliasing [3,1].

Plural is implemented as an Eclipse plugin, and can calculate permissions across all references in entire programs via a flow-sensitive analysis. Then, methods specifications in terms of permissions and typestates can be checked against the actual behavior of objects' client code. For example, a file close method has specification such as:

```
class File { ...
 @Full{requires = "open", ensures = "close"}
 public void close{};
}
```

The key contribution of this work is that its access permissions combine both aliasing and typestate information. The annotation on the close() method states both that a "@Full" permission is required—this reference may read and write, other references may read (OIRWW̄ [7])—and that the method must be called in the "open" typestate and changes the object to the "closed" typestate. (Note that Java annotations are used to encode specifications, rather than extended comments.)

## 6  Future

It appears that the community working on aliasing and ownership has reached critical mass, if the number of submissions, participants, and presentations are any indication. Consequently, we plan to repeat the workshop in conjunction with ECOOP 2009.

## References

1. Beckman, N., Bierhoff, K., Aldrich, J.: Verifying correct usage of atomic blocks and typestate. In: Kiczales, G. (ed.) Object-Oriented Programing, Systems, Languages, and Applications (OOPSLA). ACM SIGPLAN Notices. ACM Press, New York (2008) (to appear)
2. Berdine, J., Calcagno, C., O'Hearn, P.W.: Smallfoot: Modular automatic assertion checking with separation logic. In: de Boer, F.S., Bonsangue, M.M., Graf, S., de Roever, W.-P. (eds.) FMCO 2005. LNCS, vol. 4111, pp. 115–137. Springer, Heidelberg (2006)

3. Bierhoff, K., Aldrich, J.: Modular typestate checking of aliased objects. In: Object-Oriented Programing, Systems, Languages, and Applications (OOPSLA). ACM SIGPLAN Notices. ACM Press, New York (2007)

4. Bierhoff, K., Aldrich, J.: PLURAL: Checking protocol compliance under aliasing. In: Demonstration in ICSE Companion, pp. 971–972 (2008)

5. Boyland, J.: Checking interference with fractional permissions. In: Cousot, R. (ed.) SAS 2003. LNCS, vol. 2694, pp. 55–72. Springer, Heidelberg (2003)

6. Boyland, J.: Why we should not add readonly to java (yet). Journal of Object Technology 5(5), 5–29 (2006)

7. Boyland, J., Noble, J., Retert, W.: Capabilities for Sharing: A Generalization of Uniqueness and Read-Only. In: Knudsen, J.L. (ed.) ECOOP 2001. LNCS, vol. 2072, p. 2. Springer, Heidelberg (2001)

8. Brookes, S.: A semantics for concurrent separation logic. Theor. Comput. Sci. 375(1-3), 227–270 (2007)

9. Clarke, D.: Object Ownership and Containment. PhD thesis, University of New South Wales (2001)

10. Clarke, D., Drossopoulou, S., Noble, J.: Aliasing, confinement, and ownership in object-oriented programming. In: Buschmann, F., Buchmann, A., Cilia, M.A. (eds.) ECOOP 2003. LNCS, vol. 3013, pp. 197–207. Springer, Heidelberg (2004)

11. Clarke, D., Drossopoulou, S., Noble, J., Wrigstad, T.: Aliasing, confinement, and ownership in object-oriented programming. In: Cebulla, M. (ed.) ECOOP-WS 2007. LNCS, vol. 4906, pp. 40–49. Springer, Heidelberg (2008)

12. Clarke, D., Wrigstad, T.: External uniqueness is unique enough. In: Cardelli, L. (ed.) ECOOP 2003. LNCS, vol. 2743, pp. 176–200. Springer, Heidelberg (2003)

13. Clarke, D.G., Potter, J.M., Noble, J.: Ownership types for flexible alias protection. In: Object-Oriented Programing, Systems, Languages, and Applications (OOPSLA). ACM SIGPLAN Notices, vol. 33(10), pp. 48–64. ACM Press, New York (1998)

14. Dietl, W., Drossopoulou, S., Müller, P.: Generic Universe Types. In: Ernst, E. (ed.) ECOOP 2007. LNCS, vol. 4609, pp. 28–53. Springer, Heidelberg (2007)

15. Dietl, W., Müller, P.: Universes: Lightweight ownership for JML. Journal of Object Technology (JOT) 4(8), 5–32 (2005)

16. Distefano, D., O'Hearn, P.W., Yang, H.: A local shape analysis based on separation logic. In: Hermanns, H., Palsberg, J. (eds.) TACAS 2006. LNCS, vol. 3920, pp. 238–252. Springer, Heidelberg (2006)

17. Distefano, D., Parkinson, M.J.: jStar: Towards practical verification for Java. In: Kiczales, G. (ed.) Object-Oriented Programing, Systems, Languages, and Applications (OOPSLA). ACM SIGPLAN Notices. ACM Press, New York (2008) (to appear)

18. Haack, C., Hurlin, C.: Separation logic contracts for a java-like language with fork/Join. In: Meseguer, J., Roşu, G. (eds.) AMAST 2008. LNCS, vol. 5140, pp. 199–215. Springer, Heidelberg (2008)

19. Hogg, J., Lea, D., Wills, A., de Champeaux, D., Holt, R.: The Geneva Convention on the treatment of object aliasing. OOPS Messenger 3(2), 11–16 (1992)

20. Leavens, G.T., Poll, E., Clifton, C., Cheon, Y., Ruby, C., Cok, D., Müller, P., Kiniry, J., Chalin, P., Zimmerman, D.M.: JML reference manual. Department of Computer Science, Iowa State University (2008), www.jmlspecs.org

21. Leino, K.R.M.: Data groups: Specifying the modification of extended state. In: Object-Oriented Programing, Systems, Languages, and Applications (OOPSLA). ACM SIGPLAN Notices, vol. 33(10), pp. 144–153 (1998)

22. Leino, K.R.M., Müller, P.: Object invariants in dynamic contexts. In: Odersky, M. (ed.) ECOOP 2004. LNCS, vol. 3086, pp. 491–516. Springer, Heidelberg (2004)
23. Liu, Y., Milanova, A.: Ownership and immutability inference for uml-based object access control. In: International Conference on Software Engineering (ICSE), pp. 323–332. IEEE Computer Society, Los Alamitos (2007)
24. Müller, P., Rudich, A.: Ownership transfer in Universe Types. In: Object-Oriented Programing, Systems, Languages, and Applications (OOPSLA), pp. 461–478. ACM Press, New York (2007)
25. Noble, J., Vitek, J., Potter, J.: Flexible alias protection. In: Jul, E. (ed.) ECOOP 1998. LNCS, vol. 1445, pp. 158–185. Springer, Heidelberg (1998)
26. Östlund, J., Wrigstad, T., Clarke, D., Åkerblom, B.: Ownership, uniqueness, and immutability. In: Paige, R., Meyer, B. (eds.) TOOLS Europe. LNBIP, vol. 11, pp. 178–197. Springer, Heidelberg (2008)
27. Parkinson, M.J.: Class invariants: the end of the road. In: IWACO (2007)
28. Parkinson, M.J., Bierman, G.: Separation logic, abstraction, and inheritance. In: Principles of Programming Languages (POPL), pp. 75–86. ACM Press, New York (2005)
29. Potanin, A., Noble, J., Clarke, D., Biddle, R.: Generic ownership for generic java. In: Cook, W. (ed.) Object-Oriented Programing, Systems, Languages, and Applications (OOPSLA). ACM SIGPLAN Notices, vol. 41(10), pp. 311–324. ACM Press, New York (2006)
30. DeLine, R., Fähndrich, M.: Typestates for objects. In: Odersky, M. (ed.) ECOOP 2004. LNCS, vol. 3086, pp. 465–490. Springer, Heidelberg (2004)
31. Zibin, Y., Potanin, A., Ali, M., Artzi, S., Kieżun, A., Ernst, M.D.: Object and reference immutability using java generics. In: European software engineering conference and foundations of software engineering (ESEC-FSE), pp. 75–84. ACM Press, New York (2007)

# A    Participants

IWACO gathered 28 participants from 8 different countries.

| | |
|---|---|
| Suad Alagic | University of Southern Maine (USA) |
| Jonathan Aldrich | Carnegie Mellon University (USA) |
| Anindya Banerjee | Kansas State University (USA) |
| Frédéric Besson | IRISA/INRIA (France) |
| John Boyland | University of Wisconsin-Milwaukee (USA) |
| Nicholas Cameron | Imperial College (UK) |
| Dave Clarke | Katholieke Universiteit Leuven (Belgium) |
| David Cunningham | Imperial College (UK) |
| Dino Distefano | University of Cambridge (UK) |
| Sophia Drossopoulou | Imperial College (UK) |
| Patrick Eugster | Purdue University (USA) |
| Adrian Fiech | Memorial University (Canada) |
| Christian Haack | Radboud University Nijmegen (The Netherlands) |
| Clément Hurlin | INRIA (France) |
| Yu David Liu | The Johns Hopkins University (USA) |
| Nicholas Matsakis | ETH Zürich (Switzerland) |
| Ana Milanova | Rensselaer Polytechnic Institute (USA) |
| Peter Müller | Microsoft Research (USA) |
| James Noble | Victoria University of Wellington (New Zealand) |
| Johan Östlund | Purdue University (USA) |
| Alex Potanin | Victoria University of Wellington (New Zealand) |
| Jan Smans | Katholieke Universiteit Leuven (Belgium) |
| Rok Strnisa | University of Cambridge (UK) |
| Alex Summers | Imperial College (UK) |
| Tiphaine Turpin | IRISA/INRIA (France) |
| Jan Vitek | Purdue University (USA) |
| Stefan Wehr | University of Freiburg (Germany) |
| Tobias Wrigstad | Purdue University (USA) |

# B    Program Committee

| | |
|---|---|
| Kevin Bierhoff | Carnegie Mellon University (USA) |
| John Boyland | University of Wisconsin-Milwaukee (USA) |
| Werner Dietl | ETH Zurich (Switzerland) |
| Manuel Fähndrich | Microsoft Research Redmond (USA) |
| Jeff Foster | University of Maryland, College Park (USA) |
| Peter Müller (chair) | Microsoft Research Redmond (USA) |
| David Naumann | Stevens Institute of Technology (USA) |
| Matthew Parkinson | University of Cambridge (UK) |
| Arnd Poetzsch-Heffter | University of Kaiserslautern (Germany) |
| Mooly Sagiv | Tel-Aviv University (Isreal) |
| Tobias Wrigstad | Purdue University (USA) |

# C  Organizers

Dave Clarke            Katholieke Universiteit Leuven (Belgium)
Sophia Drossopoulou    Imperial College (UK)
James Noble            Victoria University of Wellington (New Zealand)
Tobias Wrigstad        Purdue University (USA)

# Implementation, Compilation, Optimization of Object-Oriented Languages, Programs and Systems

## Report on the 3rd Workshop ICOOOLPS at ECOOP 2008

Eric Jul[1] and Ian Rogers[2]

[1] DIKU, Denmark
[2] University of Manchester, UK

**Abstract.** ICOOOLPS'2008 was the third edition of the ICOOOLPS workshop at ECOOP. ICOOOLPS intends to bring researchers and practitioners both from academia and industry together, with a spirit of openness, to try and identify and begin to address the numerous and very varied issues of optimization. After two very successful editions, this third put a stronger emphasis on exchanges and discussions amongst the participants, progressing on the bases set previous years in Nantes and Berlin. The workshop attendance was relatively successful: There was about 20 attendees which was good considering the remote location and that the general attendance of ECOOP was much lower than expected. Some of the discussions (e.g., much of the afternoon sessions) were so successful that they would required even more time than we were able to dedicate to them. That is one area we plan to further improve yet again for the next edition.

## 1 Objectives and Call for Papers

Programming languages, especially object-oriented ones, are pervasive and play a significant role in computer science and engineering life. They sometime appear as ubiquitous and completely mature. However, despite a large number of works, there is still a clear need for solutions for efficient implementation and compilation of OO languages in various application domains ranging from embedded and real-time systems to desktop systems.

The ICOOOLPS workshop series thus aims to address this crucial issue of optimization in OO languages, programs and systems. It intends to do so by bringing together researchers and practitioners working in the field of object-oriented languages implementation and optimization. Its main goals are identifying fundamental bases and key current issues pertaining to the efficient implementation, compilation and optimization of OO languages, and outlining future challenges and research directions.

Topics of interest for ICOOOLPS include but are not limited to:

- implementation of fundamental OOL features:
  - inheritance (object layout, late binding, subtype test...)
  - genericity (parametric types)
  - memory management

P. Eugster (Ed.): ECOOP 2008 Workshop Reader, LNCS 5475, pp. 42–50, 2009.

- runtime systems:
  - compilers
  - linkers
  - virtual machines
- optimizations:
  - static and dynamic analyses
  - adaptive virtual machines
- resource constraints:
  - real-time systems
  - embedded systems (space, low power)...
- relevant choices and tradeoffs:
  - constant time vs. non-constant time mechanisms
  - separate compilation vs. global compilation
  - dynamic loading vs. global linking
  - dynamic checking vs. proof-carrying code
  - annotations vs. no annotations

This workshop thus tries to identify fundamental bases and key current issues pertaining to the efficient implementation and compilation of languages, especially OO ones, in order to spread them further amongst the various computing systems. It is also intended to extend this synthesis to encompass future challenges and research directions in the field of OO languages implementation and optimization.

Finally, as stated from the very beginning and the very first edition in Nantes in 2006, ICOOOLPS is intended to be a recurrent workshop in ECOOP. Because the feedback from first year attendants was very positive, and the second edition was also a great success, this third edition was set up. We integrated most of the suggestions for improvements made in 2006 and 2007, so as to further improve the workshop. The main adaptation was that less time was given to presentations, in order to free extra time for discussions.

To increase the background upon which the discussions could be based and to keep them focused, each prospective participant was encouraged to submit either a short paper describing ongoing work or a position paper describing an open issue, likely solutions, drawbacks of current solutions or alternative solutions to well known problems. Papers had to be written in English and their final version could not exceed 8 pages in LNCS style (4 pages recommended).

## 2   Organizers

**Olivier ZENDRA (chair)**,   INRIA-LORIA, Nancy, France.

|          |                              |
|----------|------------------------------|
| Email:   | olivier.zendra@inria.fr      |
| Web:     | http://www.loria.fr/~zendra  |
| Address: | INRIA / LORIA                |
|          | 615 Rue du Jardin Botanique  |
|          | BP 101                       |
|          | 54602 Villers-Ls-Nancy Cedex, FRANCE |

Olivier Zendra is a full-time permanent computer science researcher at IN-RIA / LORIA, in Nancy, France. His research topics cover compilation, optimization and automatic memory management. He worked on the compilation and optimization of object-oriented languages and was one of the two people who created and implemented SmartEiffel, The GNU Eiffel Compiler (at the time SmallEiffel). His current research topics and application domains are program analysis, compilation, memory management and embedded systems, with a specific focus on low energy.

**Eric JUL (co-chair),**          DIKU, Copenhagen, Denmark.
    Email:      eric@diku.dk
    Web:        http://www.diku.dk/~eric
    Address:    DIKU
                Universitetsparken 1
                DK-2100 Kbenhavn , DANMARK

Eric Jul is Professor of Computer Science at the University of Copenhagen and head of the Distributed Systems Group. He is one of the principal designers of the distributed, object-oriented language Emerald. He implemented fine-grained object mobility in Emerald. His current research is in Grid Computing. He is currently Vice-President of AITO.

**Roland DUCOURNAU,**                LIRMM, Montpellier, France.
    Email:      ducour@lirmm.fr
    Web:        http://www.lirmm.fr/~ducour
    Address:    LIRMM,
                161, rue Ada
                34392 Montpellier Cedex 5, FRANCE

Roland Ducournau is Professor of Computer Science at the University of Montpellier. In the late 80s, while with Sema Group, he designed and developed the YAFOOL language, based on frames and prototypes and dedicated to knowledge based systems. His research topics focuses on class specialization and inheritance, especially multiple inheritance. His recent works are dedicated to implementation of OO languages.

**Richard JONES,**              University of Kent, Canterbury, UK.
    Email:      R.E.Jones@kent.ac.uk
    Web:        http://www.cs.kent.ac.uk/~rej
    Address:    Richard Jones, Reader in Computer Systems,
                Computing Laboratory,
                University of Kent at Canterbury,
                Canterbury CT2 7NF, UK

Richard Jones is Reader in Computer Systems and Deputy Director of the Computing Laboratory at the University of Kent, Canterbury. He leads the Systems

Research Group. He is best known for his work on garbage collection: his monograph Garbage Collection remains the definitive book on the subject. His memory management research interests include techniques for avoiding space leaks, scalable yet complete garbage collection for distributed systems, flexible techniques for capturing traces of program behaviour, and heap visualisation. He was made a Distinguished Scientist of the Association for Computer Machinery (ACM) in 2006 and awarded an Honorary Fellowship at the University of Glasgow in 2005.

**Mark van den BRAND,**        Eindhoven University of Technology
                               The Netherlands

Mark van den Brand is a full professor of Software Engineering and Technology at the Eindhoven University of Technology (TU/e) in the Department of Mathematics and Computer Science. Furthermore he is scientific director of the research laboratory LaQuSo. His current research activities are on generic language technology, source code analysis, and model driven engineering. He was one of the architects of the ASF+SDF Meta-Environment (www.asfsdf.org), an integrated development environment for writing (programming) language specifications. ASF+SDF is used in the fields of language prototyping and reverse engineering.

**Stephan DUCASSE,**           NRIA Lille - Nord Europe, France

He spent ten years co-leading the Software Composition Group of the University of Bern with Prof. O. Nierstrasz. Since September 2007 he is research director at INRIA-Lille. His fields of interests are: reflective systems, meta-programming, meta-object protocols, reengineering of object-oriented applications, program visualization, maintenance, dynamic languages, language design. He is involved in the development of Squeak an open-source Smalltalk and he is the president of the European Smalltalk User Group. He wrote a couple of fun books to teach programming and other serious topics.

**Ian ROGERS,**               University of Manchester, UK

Ian Rogers is a Research Fellow in the University of Manchester's Advanced Processor Technology research group. His PhD research work in to the Dynamite binary translator was exploited commercially and now forms part of many binary translator products, including Apple's Rosetta. His recent academic work has been in to programming language design, runtime and virtual machine environments - in particular how to allow them to automatically create and efficiently exploit parallelism. He is a leading contributor to the Jikes Research Virtual Machine, where he serves as a core team member.

**Yannis SMARAGDAKIS**,        University of Oregon, USA.

Yannis Smaragdakis is an Associate Professor at the University of Oregon. His interests are in the areas of applied programming languages and software engineering. He got his B.S. degree from the University of Crete (Greece) and his Ph.D. from the University of Texas at Austin. He is a recipient of an NSF Career award, and "best paper" awards at ASE'07, ISSTA'06, GPCE'04, and USENIX'99. Yannis has authored numerous publications, and claims that "some of them are even good".

## 3   Participants

ICOOOLPS attendance was limited to 30 people for technical reasons. Unlike in the 2007 edition, it was mandatory for ICOOOLPS 2008 participants to submit a paper. Attendance at ECOOP was down this year – perhaps due to the economic situation, perhaps because of the remote location. A total of 18 people from 11 countries participated compared to the 2007 attendance of 27 people from 12 countries and the 2006 attendance of 22 people from 8 countries The attendees are listed in table 1.

**Table 1.** ICOOOLPS 2008 list of attendees

| First name | NAME | Affiliation | Country |
|---|---|---|---|
| Yuji | CHIBA | Hitachi | Japan |
| Iulian | DRAGOS | EPFL | Switzerland |
| Roland | DUCOURNAU | LIRMM | France |
| Eric | JUL | DIKU | Denmark |
| Stein | KROGDAHL | Oslo University | Norway |
| Alex | HOLKNER | RMIT University | Australia |
| Matte | LOCHAN | TU Braunschweig | Germany |
| Arne | MAUS | Oslo University | Norway |
| Anders Bach | NIELSEN | University of Århus | Denmark |
| Hridesh | RAJAN | Iowa State University | USA |
| Ian | ROGERS | University of Manchester | United Kingdom |
| Christophe | SCHOLLIERS | VUB | Belgium |
| Jaroslav | SEVIC | University of Edinburgh | United Kingdom |
| Muhammad Rabee | SHAHEEN | IMAG | France |
| Mark | VAN DEN BRAND | TU Eindhoven | The Netherlands |
| Jan | VITEK | Purdue University | USA |
| Wieger | WESSELINK | TU Eindhoven | The Netherlands |
| Xin | ZHAN | Intel | USA |

## 4   Contributions

Here are the main contributions for the sessions. More details (papers, presentations slides, etc.) are available from `http://icooolps.loria.fr`. The notes are presented here in a lively an rather informal way, so as to keep some of the spontaneity of the workshop, with of course extra organization. The notes were taken by Ian Rogers.

## 4.1   Paper 1. Coloring in Incremental Compilation of Object-Oriented Languages

Presentation by Roland Ducournau of the tradeoffs in implementing multiple inheritance Colouring presented as a desirable technique, but how to handle shared libraries and dynamic loading. Present approach to adapt technique with at worst case quadratic space overhead.

## 4.2   Paper 2. Approaches to Reflective Method Invocation

Ian Rogers presents - no notes due to presenting.

## 4.3   Paper 3. Precomputing Method Lookup

Eric Jul presents Emerald, object-oriented language for distributed systems with dynamic loading dynamic loading makes method lookup expensive, ideally would precompute method dispatch at compile time AbCon (Abstract to Concrete) mapping generated and copied by assignments. May add overhead for polymorphic objects, but in practice allows efficient dispatch.

Discussion: Method lookup, reflection and dispatch techniques No specific discussion on any one subject, some discussion of projects like steamloom and HotSpot were made.

## 4.4   Paper 4. Cast Elimination for Containers in Java

Yuji Chiba presents Moving Hitachi JRE from Java 1.5 to 1.6 was considered too much work How to improve SpecJBB performance by 10Approach to create specialised container classes. Questions/discussion: relationship to work with the pizza compiler and comparison with generics and templates, can the approach be applied within modules/globally.

## 4.5   Paper 5. The Use of a Pure Method Attribute in a Dynamic Compilation Environment

Ian Rogers presents - no notes due to presenting.

## 4.6   Paper 6. Optimizing Higher-Order Functions in Scala

Iulian Dragos presented. The compilation of Scala was explained with details on the inefficiencies. Optimizations that are specific to Scala were detailed Preliminary benchmarks results were presented demonstrating a 3646

### 4.7    Paper 7. C++ Move Semantics for Exception Safety and Optimization in Software Transactional Memory Libraries

No presenter was available, some discussion about what the paper was about was had.

### 4.8    Paper 8. Boot Image Layout for Jikes RVM

Ian Rogers presents - no notes due to presenting.

### 4.9    Discussion Session: Memory Management, Is It That Important?

Define terminology, such as imprecise GC What is real-time GC? - Real-Time Specification for Java (RTSJ) - based on regions. Real-time GC - does it work? - worst case pause time can be 400ms, therefore twice as slow. Real-time problem demo. Discussion of train algorithm for real-time GC. Disscussion of whether or not we need defragmentation of the heap. Jan Vitek gives presentation of work with Fil Pizlo:

- discussion of manual memory techniques for real-time.
- scoped memory - use of nesting, runtime checks, Sun's use of RTSJ
- real-time shouldn't kill performance.
- Jamaica VM - work based adding cost to allocate and read.
- Henrikson/Sun - slack based, needs preemptible GC - rollback on preemption aborting copy, but can lead to priority inversion.
- Metronome - time based approach.
- rough IBM DK performance figures of 18x slowdown for scoped.

memory and 3x for time based approach. Discussion of how these systems are used in an aeroplane? Run 3 times with worst-case analysis, how? Discussion on what is the effect of stack allocation on real-time techniques? Discussion of work on non-blocking concurrent collectors in PLDI '08. Discussion on what is the effect of multi-cores on GC.

### 4.10    Discussion Session: Java in Embedded Systems

Discussion of embedded systems and environments available, for example Lego mindstorms nxt has virutal machine (originally with no GC), Scheme interpreter for ARM, it's possible to program in a C style on a Lego mindstorms. What is embedded (mindstorms 256kb vs embedded Java ¡ 32MB)? Discussion of sensor networks, reliability is important, SunSpots allow sensor networks with JVMs. Discussion of possible static compilation routes for Java. Discussion of overheads of Java for embedded devices, memory. footprint, power consumption, how to access embedded registers.

### 4.11    Discussion. Do Threads Make Sense?

Discussion of common sub-expression elimination being invalid with volatiles How should concurrent code be created? Increased use of java.util.concurrent. Discussion of co-routines in Simula. Discussion, what is Java missing for concurrency? Emerald has immutable/frozen objects, unfreezing (as in Ruby) wouldn't be desirable due to problems with semantics (as with the problem of finalizers and weak references in Java).

## 5    Conclusion

This third edition of ICOOOLPS was a successful successor to the previous two. Despite the reduced attendance at ECOOP, we still had our fair share of participants – and enough to make for some very interesting discussion.

This clearly bides well for the future and the building of a small, informal, community.

On a more scientific level, once again thanks to the skills of the speakers and active participation of the attendants, the discussions were lively, open-minded and allowed good exchanges. We had allocated more time for discussions than last year, but it was barely enough.

Another encouraging aspect is that some discussions (garbage collection, Java threads) recurred from 2006 and 2007, which shows there is interesting work to be done in these areas.

As we had mentioned last year identifying the main challenges for optimization is not that easy, if only because optimizations for object-oriented languages come in variety of contexts with very different constraints (embedded, real-time, dynamic, legacy...) hence different optimizations criteria (speed, size, memory footprint, energy...). One thing that emerged more clearly in this third edition is the fact that some of our concerns extend beyond object-oriented languages (to functional languages, for example). Another important point is that to optimize, it is difficult to consider separately implementation and language design, or at least specifications.

## 6    Perspectives: ICOOOLPS Future

The ICOOOLPS PC members present held a short organization meeting after the workshop.

Some concern over drop in attendance (consistent with drop in ECOOP 2008 attendance). Difficulties for PC members to come to Paphos (cost, inconvenient travel) was cited. Difficulties due to the Chair, Olivier, was unable to attend – Eric took over. One presenter had passport/visa problems and could not show up. Ian Rogers volunteered to help in organizing the next edition – and was promptly chosen as Chair – with support from Eric, who volunteered to be co-chair.

Like every year, we try to draw lessons from each edition to further improve the following ICOOOLPS editions. This year, we noted several aspects to improve, amongst which the main ones are:

- This year, we had shorter presentations and longer discussions than in 2006 and 2007. That was good. In 2009 we should *devote at least as much time to discussions* as in 2008, with an emphasis on short presentations: the purpose of a workshop is not papers, but brainstorming. Presentations should be 10 minutes *max* + 10 minutes for questions.
- We must be *very strict with presentations times*, and not hesitate to stop a speaker who is exceeding her/his time.
- The *papers* do have to be available on the website *before* the workshop.
- Session report drafts should be written during a session (papers and talks) and maybe briefly discussed at the end of each session (not after the workshop). Session scribes should be chosen beforehand.
- Prior registration with the workshop organizers, like in ICOOOLPS 2006, is better. It helps keeping track of attendants, gathering their topics of interest, etc.
- We had good experience with asking for *a list of suggested discussion topics* at registration time, so that attendees can vote for them (or suggest new ones).

Of course, some of these points put an increased burden on the organizers, but are key to an even more successful and enjoyable workshop.

We also intend to selectively enlarge the audience to other — possibly non-OO — communities who face the same kind of issues as the one we focus on in ICOOOLPS.

## 7   Background

To provide a fixed access point for ICOOOLPS related matters, the web site for the workshop is maintained at `http://icooolps.loria.fr`. All the papers and presentations done for ICOOOLPS'2008 are freely available there.

# Aspects, Dependencies and Interactions
## Report on the 3rd Workshop ADI at ECOOP 2008

Frans Sanen[1], Katharina Mehner[2], Ruzanna Chitchyan[3],
Lodewijk Bergmans[4], Johan Fabry[5], and Mario Sudholt[6]

[1] K.U. Leuven, Leuven, Belgium
frans.sanen@cs.kuleuven.be
[2] Siemens, Germany
Katharina.Mehner@siemens.com
[3] Lancaster University, Lancaster, UK
rouza@comp.lancs.ac.uk
[4] University of Twente, Enschede, The Netherlands
L.M.J.Bergmans@ewi.utwente.nl
[5] Computer Science Department (DCC), University of Chile
jfabry@dcc.uchile.cl
[6] Ecole des Mines de Nantes, Nantes, France
Mario.Sudholt@emn.fr

**Abstract.** The topics on aspects, dependencies and interactions are among the key remaining challenges to be tackled by the Aspect-Oriented Software Development (AOSD) community to enable a wide adoption of AOSD technology. This third workshop, organized and supported by the AOSD-Europe project, aimed to continue the wide discussion on aspects, dependencies and interactions started at ADI 2006 and continued at ADI 2007.

**Keywords:** Aspects, dependencies, interactions.

## 1 Introduction

Interaction problems between different modules, program parts, units of specifications are a central challenge to many program structuring paradigms, including Aspect-Oriented Software Development, feature-based programming and component-based software engineering. Furthermore, interaction problems are relevant to all phases of the software development life cycle: from requirements through to implementation and often exert a broad influence on these concerns, e.g. by modifying their semantics, structure and / or behavior. Such dependencies often lead to both desirable and unwanted or unexpected behaviors of large-scale applications. The workshop was focused on identifying, understanding, and resolving all kinds of issues related to such dependencies and interactions, by bringing together researchers and practitioners from across the whole spectrum of software development activities and methodologies. The goal of this third workshop was to continue the wide discussion on aspects, dependencies and

P. Eugster (Ed.): ECOOP 2008 Workshop Reader, LNCS 5475, pp. 51–62, 2009.

interactions, started at ADI 2006 and continued at ADI 2007, thus investigating the lasting nature of such dependency links across all development activities:

- starting from the early development stages (i.e., requirements, architecture, and design), looking into dependencies between requirements (e.g., positive/negative contributions between aspectual goals) and interactions caused by aspects (e.g., quality attributes) in requirements, architecture, and design;
- analyzing these dependencies and interactions both through modeling and formal analysis;
- considering language design issues which help to handle such dependencies and interactions;
- studying such interactions in applications.

In the rest of this workshop report, we present the main topics that were discussed at the workshop, including a comparative overview of the main topics of the accepted papers, a summary of the keynote speech by James Noble on "We Demand Rigidly Defined Areas of Doubt and Uncertainty!", a summing-up of the debates hold in the discussion breakout group and a synthesis of the panel chaired by Theo D'Hondt on "Does Model Driven Engineering make Aspects Obsolete?"

## 2    Accepted Papers

Papers accepted to the workshop covered a broad spectrum of problems related to aspects, dependencies and interactions. We have clustered these papers into three sets, with each set briefly summarized below.

### 2.1    Architecture

This set of papers focuses mainly on architecture, namely the management of aspect interactions using statically-verified control-flow relations and analyzing layering violations in aspect-oriented software architectures.

In [10], the feasibility of a technique for managing control-flow interactions in layered architectures is demonstrated. The technique proposes to document aspects with policies that specify the expected control-flow relations between different aspects or between aspects and the base application. The policies are expressed as logic formulae that employ a set of predicates that represent relevant control-flow situations. In order to verify these policies, the authors employ and extend existing static analyses to produce interprocedural control-flow graphs of an application with woven aspects. This graph then is traversed in a controlled manner to characterize the realizable paths. The paper starts with the observation that although various aspect-oriented approaches provide support for the management of aspect interactions, most techniques are only applicable when the aspects share a common join point (e.g. [7,8,19]). However, De Fraine et al. motivate that aspect interactions also occur on coarser levels based on two example interactions between the following three aspects in a typical multi-tier architecture: authorization, authentication and caching. E.g. caching should not override the authorization behavior since the caching aspect can skip the normal operation by returning a previous result from the cache instead of applying a authorization check. Based on these example interactions, the authors identify a need for expressing control-flow policies that are able to express control-flow relations such as "occurs in all paths" or "cannot remove invocations of" between aspects or aspects and the base. To summarize, their integrated technique to manage control-flow interactions consists of three steps: (1) static analysis of application code with woven aspects to produce an abstraction of the possible control-flow paths in the resulting application, (2) formal documentation of aspects with control-flow policies that specify the relations that aspects depend on and (3) an algorithm to detect violations of control-flow policies in the abstract paths produced as the result of the static analysis.

In [16], the authors present a study with the goal of analyzing the influence of aspect-orientation on violations of the layered structure of software architectures. They argue that existing metrics for layering violations do not appropriately accommodate the notion of aspects. The need to extend the suite of metrics to allow more precise quantative evaluations of layering violations when aspects are involved is discussed. The paper observes the fact that although many assessments of AOP have conducted in the last few years (e.g. [9,15]), only a small number of studies addresses specifically its impact on the architecture of a software system. The work that is described in the paper concerns a study on the impact of AOP techniques on layered software architectures. The empirical study targets five evolution scenarios of a real-life web-based information system, called Health Watcher. The paper focuses its analysis on layering violations. Layering violations are defined as situations when a layer is a client to another layer that is not below it or not adjacent to it. The different categories of layering violations they distinguish are termed skip-call, back-call and cyclic dependency. In their architectural layer violation measurement framework, they start with (automatically) identifying all the dependencies between modules (method calls, field access, field assignment and exception handling). Next, a metrics collection step is carried out to detect layering violations. This step works as follows: for each dependency between a module A and B, the corresponding layer in which they are located is determined. It then checks whether A's layer is higher than B's layer and if A and B are adjacent. The paper finally presents some preliminary numbers evaluating the architectural layering principles for the different Health Watcher evolution scenariosw.

## 2.2   Types and Semantics

This set of papers looks at type restriction of around advice and aspect interference on the one hand and formal semantics of distributed aspects and invasive patterns based on labeled transition systems on the other hand.

In [14], a novel weaving mechanism is presented called type relaxed weaving. Type relaxed weaving allows advice applications while preserving type safety. The problem with statically typed AOP languages (e.g. AspectJ), where applications of around advice only are allowed to join points with conforming types, is that they possibly prohibit applying useful advices. They clarify the problem by using the notion of the most specific usage type of a value. The usage type of a value is its static parameter or receiver type when that value is used as a parameter or a receiver of a method respectively. The most specific usage type of a value is a type T such that T is a subtype of any usage type of the value. The basic idea behind the type relaxed weaving is that the original AspectJ rules need to be extended with the rule "For each join point matching a pointcut P, type T must be a subtype of its most specific usage type of its return value". The paper also discusses several design issues that need to be addressed in order to realize the type relaxed weaving. For example, how to approach the usage type of an overridden method call or what to do when usage types don't match? In addition, it is argued that when aspects interact via advice declarations that are applicable to the same join point, care must be taken about type safety. Before the paper is concluded, a preliminary feasibility assessment is given.

In [17], two formal semantics based on labeled transition systems are presented for distributed aspects in AWED [18] and invasive patterns that should enable the definition of interaction properties of aspects and pattern compositions. Invasive patterns are an extension of standard parallel and distributed architectural patterns for complex distributed algorithms. After a short overview of the AWED language, the pattern language is discussed. Basically, it uses a pattern constructor patternSeq that takes as argument a list G1 A1 G2 A2 ... Gn of alternating group and aspect definitions. Each triple Gi Ai Gi+1 in this list corresponds to a pattern application that uses the aspect Ai to trigger the pattern in a source group Gi and realizes effects in the set of target hosts Gi+1. A group G is either defined as a set of host identifiers or through a pattern constructor term itself. The language constructs are formally defined in terms of labeled transition systems. These definitions can be analyzed with existing model checkers. Finally, the authors show that these semantics can be used to check certain liveness and safety properties.

## 2.3   Model-Driven Development

This set of papers addresses handling crosscutting concerns in model-driven software development, thus investigating the combination of aspect-oriented and model-driven software development approaches.

In [1], an approach to create model-driven software product lines is presented including fine-variations. Fine-variations of model-driven software product lines correspond to characteristics that affect particular elements of models involved in the model transformations. For example, it should be possible in a domotics system to select light components that possess the functionality of automatic lights *on a per instance basis*. In addition, these instances can be configured individually (behave differently) based on different attributes (time and infrared presence detection for instance). Such fine-grained variations are an important activity in the SPL process, e.g. to derive a correctly customized product. The proposed approach improves on the AO-MD-SPL approach as originally presented by Voelter et al. [21] and uses feature models, constraint models (constraints being relations between features and metaconcepts to restrict specific choices for a product) and fine-feature configurations (expressed between features and model elements). Hence, products are configured creating fine-feature configurations and based on these configurations, model-driven software product lines are created using aspect-oriented principles. The authors claim that, as a result, their approach allows to derive products including fine-grained details of configuration.

In [3], DiVA [6] is presented. DiVA's goal is to provide a new tool-supported methodology with an integrated framework for managing dynamic variability in adaptive systems. In order to address this goal, aspect-oriented and model-driven techniques will be combined in an innovative way. The idea behind this combination is that models cope with complexity through abstracting over the dynamic variability and that AO techniques are used to model the adaptation concerns separately from other aspects of the system. On the one hand, DiVA proposes to use models at two levels (i.e. design time and run time) in order to manage dynamic variability. On the other hand, aspect-oriented modelling techniques allows them to tackle the issue of the combinatorial explosion of variants. The combination of these model-based abstractions and advanced separation of concerns enables adaptations that can be easier designed, understood, validated and evolved. DiVA uses industrial case studies from two different domains to validate the proposed approach: crisis management at an airport and a customer relationship management system.

In [12], a brief description is given of GReCCO, an aspect-oriented modeling-based framework to promote and enhance the reuse of concerns. GReCCo supports (1) composition obliviousness by modelling concerns independently from a concrete context in which they are going to be applied, (2) composition symmetry by treating all concerns (including the base concern) uniformly, and (3) interdependency management by a coupling to the Concern Interaction Acquisition (CIA) system [20]. The authors have developed a prototype composition engine implemented in ATL that can be used to compose concern models specified in UML. W.r.t. (1), concern models are used to describe both structure and behavior of concerns using UML class and sequence diagrams respectively. In addition, a composition model describes how the source concern models should be composed. In this composition specification, model elements can be added, modified, removed, merged and instantiated. For overlapping behavior scenarios, an ordering is derived. The output of the symmetric composition engine (2) is a composed model from the input composition and the concern models.

## 3   Keynote Speech by James Noble on "We Demand Rigidly Defined Areas of Doubt and Uncertainty!"

A key idea behind aspect-oriented software development is that software cannot be described by tree structures such as OO designs, nested abstractions or layered virtual machines. Unfortunately, this means that the topologies of the software we build, and the interactions within those topologies, will be more complex than we once hoped. The work presented in this keynote presented a philosophical context for this analysis, showed how a range of research fits into in that context, and attempted to outline some future directions. The keynote surveyed the work of many and aimed explicitly at raising questions rather than providing answers.

The keynote started with an interesting observation of where the software engineering community is at this point. This observation started with an example where next to a functional concern also security, transactional and exception handling issues were involved. In this example, the AOSD promise (*offering an alternative to the current state of low cohesion and implicit coupling in programming due to tangled and scattered concerns*) holds. In concreto, obliviousness can increase cohesion and quantification typically decreases coupling (both together referred to by the speaker as *the mess we're in*). In what followed, Pascal's triangle (named after Blaise Pascal) was used to focus on interactions and dependencies. Assuming every program can be represented as a tree (whatever programming language is used), aspect-orientation programming can be seen as factoring different crosscutting concerns out of such a hierarchical model, with higher cohesion as a result. Dependencies and interactions then boil down to the different relationships that exist and remain to be managed between these aspects that are factored out. *Should we pay every price to get a higher cohesion in return* was the open question that ended this starting observation.

In what followed, everything got placed in a broader philosophical perspective and the audience was referred to the notorious werewolf (i.e. personification of failure in software projects), introduced by Brooks at the beginning of his well-known *No silver bullet* article [4] on essential versus accidental complexity. Essential complexity refers to a situation where all reasonable solutions to a problem must be complicated (and possibly confusing) because the "simple" solutions would not adequately solve the problem. Accidental complexity on the other hand might arise purely from mismatches in the particular choice of tools and methods applied in the solution. For decades, software construction consisted of a sequence of refinement steps. In each step, a given task is broken up into a number of subtasks and each refinement implies a number of design decisions. In a more general context, these times of modernism and modernity were characterized by the belief in a *Grand Narrative*, progress via abstraction, regularity of structure and supremacy of science and history. However, postmodernism brought an end to this: *Grand Narratives* collapsed, negotiation and context gained tremendously in importance, different topologies emerged and reuse became a laudable goal. In the mean time, *small narratives* had proven to superbly allow for imaginative invention. Decisions rather are a result of a trial and error process instead of a well-defined step-by-step process. During the trial and error process, negotiation is needed between various narratives, the context becomes more and more important and it's possible that no single correct answer exists. The speaker discussed a couple of examples that perfectly fit in this postmodern mindset, such as for example design patterns [11]. Design patterns are small stories that resolve a specific problem locally. As soon as one starts putting different design patterns together, negotation becomes inevitable. The philosophical context applied to AO gives poses the following interesting points:

- Objects are the basic components.
- Aspects are the crosscutting components. In addition, each aspect is a small, independent part.
- Aspect interactions are essentially complex.
- Aspects negotiate to provide or overrule each other's behaviour.

The last part of the talk concluded by stating that aspect dependencies and interactions are one of the essential (not accidental) complexities in aspect-oriented software engineering. Reasoning about dependencies and interactions therefore should happen in a local, provisional way. Negotiation can then be used to constrain module configurations or module interactions (or both). In other words, we need... rigidly defined areas of doubt and uncertainty.

# 4   Discussion Topics

One of the sessions of the workshop was devoted to a group discussion. This group discussion is summarized below. We first present a high-level, overall summary of the entire group discussion session. A detailed example is discussed below.

## 4.1   Overall Summary

During the group discussion session of the ADI 2008 workshop, we have talked about a set of approaches proposed so far, that aim at discovering different kinds of dependencies and interactions in AO programs such as [10,16,5,22,8]. We have observed during our discussions that such approaches shared a set of common characteristics, and adopted a very similar high-level structure.

1. They usually depend on a program representation - which can be the program source code or bytecode or any other intermediate representation such as for example the program control flow graph (CFG).
2. Next, they represent the set of relations they are interested in finding as a set of rules - such rules can be represented in semi-structured languages such as XML or logical expressions.
3. Finally, they traverse the program representation checking such rules. They go through the program representation and perform a kind of pattern matching algorithm looking for the relationships that may arise among the components of which the program is composed.

## 4.2   Detailed Example

One of the works discussed was the work described in [5]. This work describes a tool called SAFE (Static Analyser for the Flow of Exceptions) that mines the interactions between aspects and classes in exception-aware systems. Most of the current programming languages provide exception mechanisms as a means to assist software developers building robust systems, allowing the separation between the normal control flow of the program and the exceptional flow. The separation between normal and exceptional flow of a program bares some consequences: for instance, it creates new dependencies between the elements that compose the system - more specifically, between the elements that signal exceptions and the elements responsible for handling them. Such tool performs a static analysis of AspectJ programs looking for the implicit and explicit dependencies that may arise between the program abstractions (aspects and classes) caused by exception handling scenarios. An advice adding new functionality to the base code can also bring new exceptional conditions due to the additional functionality. Such exceptions will flow until they are handled somewhere in the code. This scenario creates a dependency between the exception-signaling aspect and the elements (on the base code or other aspects) on which the exception is handled. This interaction-finding approache works on java bytecode, enables the user to define which elements are responsible for signalling and handle exceptions in XML files (i.e., a ser of rules), and than traverses the code finding the signaller-handler relationships and checking whether the rules are obeyed by them.

## 5    Panel on "Does Model-Driven Engineering Make Aspects Obsolete?"

The workshop hosted a panel that discussed the question "Does Model-Driven Engineering Make Aspects Obsolete?". The panelists were Stephan Herrmann, Shigeru Chiba, Hidehiko Masuhara and Wolfgang De Meuter. The panel was chaired by Theo D'Hondt. In what follows. we first elaborate concisely on the different panel positions in which each of the four panelists presented his personal view on the matter. Next, a short overview is given from the panel discussion based on questions from the workshop attendants.

### 5.1    Panel Positions

*Hidehiko Masuhara* started by declaring that he is not really a model-driven engineering (MDE) specialist. As a consequence, he preferred to take a rather neutral position in this panel. *Shigeru Chiba* declared that aspects can be a tool for implementing program transformations in MDE. Therefore, he proposed to add a footnote to the title of the panel reflecting this: "For model-driven engineering to be practical, AOP is a program transformation tool". *Stephan Herrman* pointed out that from a definition point of view, aspects are inferior to MDE: the latter research community consists of the real experts in program transformations that possibly are customizable to different domains. Aspects originally were defined as a weaving technology, being only one kind of program transformation. A final point he made in the beginning of the panel is that we only need two hands for counting the problems that can be solved by aspects. On the contrary, good frameworks exist that solve exactly these problems and that can be used in combination with domain-specific languages to weave these frameworks into the application. If we indeed assume that from a definition point of view, MDE is superior, we should ask ourselves what can be saved from aspects? *Wolfgang De Meuter* stated that he does not really believe in model-driven engineering. He suggested that aspects are there and always will be. The question that remains, according to him, is how we can and will realize them in our programming languages.

## 5.2   Panel Discussion

Discussions were centered around two more specific topics: aspects versus models and the role of transformations. Summaries for both these discussions are provided below.

**Aspects versus models.** The workshop participants agreed that they didn't experience aspects versus models as much competing as the panelists's statements might suggest. To start with, the audience pointed out that there still is no really good, broadly acknowledged definition of *an aspect*. Definitions exist in nearly all software development lifecycle phases and no single definition exists where everybody agrees upon. Time seems to have proven that aspects are most useful at an implementation level, while MDE rather focuses at the earlier lifecycle phases. Stephan Herrmann repeated his thoughts about the context we are in now: a context where a lot of code is already there as frameworks, libraries, etc. Any MDE approach that generates code for such a platform of frameworks and libraries leverages this wealth of existing software in a way that is not easily accessible by using mainstream AOP. Shigeru Chiba referred back to the invited speech of James Noble at the beginning of this workshop, in which the speaker indicated that we are tired with tree structures. Hence, aspects can represent a new way of thinking (and not only an implementation technique) and can serve as a kind of abstraction.

In a lively discussion hereafter, the real contribution of MDE was discussed upon. Is it the machinery of meta-modeling and easy tooling of transformations and new modeling languages? An obvious contribution is that (in theory) one is able, for each purpose, to use the most appropriate modeling mechanism and machinery that will produce code. For real software, a Turing complete programming language is needed; does the same hold for the modeling language and can the latter become as complex as the programming language? Does MDE subsume everything or in other words, can everything in AOP also be done in MDE, potentially in a more convenient way? AOP needs rescuing? And if so, should we look where MDE fails and can we use aspects to solve what remains to be done? How can we capture a crosscutting concern in MDE and how can we compose it in such an approach? Are there any satisfactory ways of specifying where a crosscutting concern is needed in one or more models yet? Does annotation-based weaving or a class diagram in combination with a table relating elements and mechanisms suffice?

**The role of transformations.** One of the panelists switched the focus of ongoing discussions to the role of transformations by provoking the audience with the following statement: "Maybe MDE generates the code that you don't have to write in a really good programming language". "MDE being most valuable when input languages significantly differ from output languages, i.e. when there is a large representation gap to be filled" countered this. Are executable models not a better alternative for the *transformation obsession*? Is the only price to pay in this case the interpreter that is required to be written for an executable model? What would be the exact differences between such an interpreter and the well-known meta-model in an MDE approach?

Different ways exist to implement model transformations. Javassist [13] for instance provides a way of describing Java bytecode transformations, but the complexity of the tool is relatively high. AspectJ [2] on the other hand offers easier, more declarative and more expressive mechanisms for expressing trans-formations, but only for rather simple concerns such as logging and persistence. A domain in which MDE has proven to be very useful is telecommunications. One of the main reasons for this is that lots of behaviour can be modelled in state charts and the developer actually does not see any code at all because it is fully generated by the compiler.

Finally, most members of the audience agreed that aspects do not have to defend their existence since they represent an advanced modularization technique that is orthogonal and complementary to models. The AO community strongly would benefit from some strong arguments where MDE falls short in comparison with AO. An important sideremark also was made: transformations might not be *the* fundamental part of a MDE process but rather an optimization.

## 6    Conclusion

This third workshop on Aspects, Dependencies and Interactions provided an opportunity for presentations and lively discussion between researchers working on AOSD, dependencies and interactions from all over the world. The workshop continued the wide discussion on aspects, dependencies and interactions that was started at ADI 2006 and continued at ADI 2007. It is our intention to continue encouraging the challenging work on this topic by further organizing a number of follow-up workshops.

## 7    Workshop Organizers and Participants

### 7.1    List of Organizers

The workshop organizing committee consisted of the following five members.

- Frans Sanen, K.U.Leuven, Belgium (co-chair)
  Email: frans.sanen (at) cs.kuleuven.be
- Mario Sudholt, Ecole des Mines de Nantes, France (co-chair)
  Email: mario.sudholt (at) emn.fr
- Ruzanna Chitchyan, Lancaster University, UK
  Email: rouza (at) comp.lancs.ac.uk
- Lodewijk Bergmans, University of Twente, The Netherlands
  Email: L.M.J.Bergmans (at) ewi.utwente.nl

– Johan Fabry, Computer Science Department (DCC), University of Chile, Chile
  Email: jfabry (at) dcc.uchile.cl
– Katharina Mehner, Siemens, Germany
  Email: Katharina.Mehner (at) siemens.com

## 7.2   List of Attendees

The list of attendees officially registered for the workshop is presented alphabetically below. It should be noted that a number of unregistered attendees also participated, but these are not listed here.

1. Shigeru Chiba (Tokyo Institute of Technology, Japan)
2. Roberta de Souza Coelho (Pontifical Catholic University of Rio de Janeiro, Brazil)
3. Bruno De Fraine (Vrije Universiteit Brussel, Belgium)
4. Wolfgang De Meuter (Vrije Universiteit Brussel, Belgium)
5. Theo D'Hondt (Vrije Universiteit Brussel, Belgium)
6. Stephan Herrmann (Technische Universitat Berlin, Germany)
7. Viviane Jonckers (Vrije Universiteit Brussel, Belgium)
8. Uira Kulesza (Pontifical Catholic University of Rio de Janeiro, Brazil)
9. Hidehiko Masuhara (University of Tokyo, Japan)
10. James Noble (Victoria University of Wellington, New Zealand)
11. Angel Nunez (Ecole des Mines de Nantes, France)
12. Eline Philips (Vrije Universiteit Brussel, Belgium)
13. Frans Sanen (K.U.Leuven, Belgium)

# References

1. Arboleda, H., Casallas, R., Royer, J.-C.: Using transformation-aspects for model-driven software product lines. In: Proceedings of the Third International Workshop on Aspects, Dependencies and Interactions (held at ECOOP), pp. 46–56 (2008)
2. AspectJ: Aspect-Oriented Java Extension, http://www.eclipse.org/aspectj/
3. Ayed, D.: Diva: Dynamic variability in complex adative systems. In: Proceedings of the Third International Workshop on Aspects, Dependencies and Interactions (held at ECOOP), pp. 57–61 (2008)
4. Brooks, F.P.: No silver bullet: Essence and accidents of software engineering. Computer 20(4), 10–19 (1987)
5. Coelho, R., Rashid, A., Garcia, A., Ferrari, F.C., Cacho, N., Kulesza, U., von Staa, A., de Lucena, C.J.P.: Assessing the impact of aspects on exception flows: An exploratory study. In: Vitek, J. (ed.) ECOOP 2008. LNCS, vol. 5142, pp. 207–234. Springer, Heidelberg (2008)
6. DiVA: Dynamic Variability in Complex, Adaptive Systems, http://www.ict-diva.eu/
7. Douence, R., Fradet, P., Südholt, M.: A framework for the detection and resolution of aspect interactions. In: Batory, D., Consel, C., Taha, W. (eds.) GPCE 2002. LNCS, vol. 2487, pp. 173–188. Springer, Heidelberg (2002)

8. Durr, P., Bergmans, L., Aksit, M.: Reasoning about semantic conflicts between aspects. In: EIWAS 2005: The 2nd European Interactive Workshop on Aspects in Software, pp. 10–18 (2005)
9. Figueiredo, E., Cacho, N., Sant'Anna, C., Monteiro, M., Kulesza, U., Garcia, A., Soares, S., Ferrari, F., Khan, S., Filho, F.C., Dantas, F.: Evolving software product lines with aspects: an empirical study on design stability. In: ICSE 2008: Proceedings of the 30th International Conference on Software Engineering, pp. 261–270. ACM, New York (2008)
10. Fraine, B.D., Quiroga, P.D., Jonckers, V.: Management of aspect interactions using statically-verified control-flow relations. In: Proceedings of the Third International Workshop on Aspects, Dependencies and Interactions (held at ECOOP), pp. 5–14 (2008)
11. Gamma, E., Helm, R., Johnson, R., Vlissides, J.: Design Patterns. Addison-Wesley Professional, Reading (1995)
12. Hovsepyan, A., Baelen, S.V., Berbers, Y., Joosen, W.: Grecco: Composing generic reusable concerns. In: Proceedings of the Third International Workshop on Aspects, Dependencies and Interactions (held at ECOOP), pp. 62–63 (2008)
13. Javassist: Java Programming Assistant, http://www.jboss.org/javassist/
14. Masuhara, H.: On type restriction of around advice and aspect interference. In: Proceedings of the Third International Workshop on Aspects, Dependencies and Interactions (held at ECOOP), pp. 15–25 (2008)
15. Molesini, A., Garcia, A.F., von Chavez Flach Garcia, C., Batista, T.V.: On the quantitative analysis of architecture stability in aspectual decompositions. In: WICSA 2008: Proceedings of the Seventh Working IEEE/IFIP Conference on Software Architecture (WICSA 2008), Washington, DC, USA, pp. 29–38. IEEE Computer Society, Los Alamitos (2008)
16. Monteiro, M., Moura, M., Soares, S., Filho, F.C.: Towards an analysis of layering violations in aspect-oriented software architectures. In: Proceedings of the Third International Workshop on Aspects, Dependencies and Interactions (held at ECOOP), pp. 26–35 (2008)
17. Navarro, L.D.B., Douence, R., Nunez, A., Sudholt, M.: Lts-based semantics and property analysis of distributed aspects and invasive patterns. In: Proceedings of the Third International Workshop on Aspects, Dependencies and Interactions (held at ECOOP), pp. 36–45 (2008)
18. Navarro, L.D.B., Südholt, M., Vanderperren, W., Fraine, B.D., Suvée, D.: Explicitly distributed aop using awed. In: AOSD 2006: Proceedings of the 5th international conference on Aspect-oriented software development, pp. 51–62. ACM, New York (2006)
19. Pawlak, R., Duchien, L., Seinturier, L.: Compar: Ensuring safe around advice composition. In: Steffen, M., Zavattaro, G. (eds.) FMOODS 2005. LNCS, vol. 3535, pp. 163–178. Springer, Heidelberg (2005)
20. Sanen, F., Truyen, E., Joosen, W.: Managing concern interactions in middleware. In: Indulska, J., Raymond, K. (eds.) DAIS 2007. LNCS, vol. 4531, pp. 267–283. Springer, Heidelberg (2007)
21. Voelter, M., Groher, I.: Product line implementation using aspect-oriented and model-driven software development. In: SPLC 2007: Proceedings of the 11th International Software Product Line Conference, Washington, DC, USA, pp. 233–242. IEEE Computer Society, Los Alamitos (2007)
22. Weston, N., Taiani, F., Rashid, A.: Interaction analysis for fault-tolerance in aspect-oriented programming. In: Proceedings of the Third International Workshop on Aspects, Dependencies and Interactions (held at ECOOP), pp. 36–45 (2008)

# Getting Farther on Software Evolution
## via AOP and Reflection
### Report on the 5th RAM-SE Workshop at ECOOP 2008

Manuel Oriol[1], Walter Cazzola[2], Shigeru Chiba[3], and Gunter Saake[4]

[1] Department of Computer Science,
University of York, York, United Kingdom
manuel@cs.york.ac.uk
[2] DICo - Department of Informatics and Communication,
Università degli Studi di Milano, Milano, Italy
cazzola@dico.unimi.it
[3] Department of Mathematical and Computing Sciences,
Tokyo Institute of Technology, Tokyo, Japan
chiba@is.titech.ac.jp
[4] Institute für Technische und Betriebliche Informationssysteme,
Otto-von-Guericke-Universität Magdeburg, Magdeburg, Germany
saake@iti.cs.uni-magdeburg.de

**Abstract.** Following last four years' RAM-SE (Reflection, AOP and Meta-Data for Software Evolution) workshop at the ECOOP conference, the RAM-SE'08 workshop was a successful and popular event. As its name implies, the workshop's focus was on the application of reflective, aspect-oriented and data-mining techniques to the broad field of software evolution. Topics and discussions at the workshop included mechanisms for supporting software evolution, technological limits of the aspect-oriented and reflective approaches to software evolution and tools devoted to software evolution.

The workshop's main goal was to bring together researchers working in the field of software evolution with a particular interest in reflection, aspect-oriented programming and meta-data. The workshop was organized as a full day meeting, partly devoted to presentation of submitted position papers and partly devoted to panel discussions about the presented topics and other interesting issues in the field. In this way, the workshop allowed participants to get acquainted with each other's work, and stimulated collaboration. We hope this helped participants in improving their ideas and the quality of their future publications.

The workshop's proceedings, including all accepted position papers can be downloaded from the workshop's web site and a post workshop proceeding, including an extension of the accepted paper is planned to be published by the University of Magdeburg.

In this report, we provide a session-by-session overview of the workshop, and then present our opinions about future trends in software evolution.

P. Eugster (Ed.): ECOOP 2008 Workshop Reader, LNCS 5475, pp. 63–69, 2009.
© Springer-Verlag Berlin Heidelberg 2009

# 1   Workshop Description and Objectives

Software evolution and adaptation is a research area that offers stimulating challenges for both academic and industrial researchers. The evolution of software systems, to face unexpected situations or just for improving their features, relies on software engineering techniques and methodologies. Nowadays a similar approach is not applicable in all situations e.g., for evolving non stopping systems or systems whose code is not available.

Features of reflection such as transparency, separation of concerns, and extensibility seem to be perfect tools to aid the dynamic evolution of running systems. Aspect-oriented programming (AOP) can simplify code instrumentation whereas techniques that rely on meta-data can be used to inspect the system and to extract the necessary data for designing the heuristic that the reflective and aspect-oriented mechanism use for managing the evolution.

We feel the necessity to investigate the benefits brought by the use of these techniques on the evolution of object-oriented software systems. In particular we would determine how these techniques can be integrated with more traditional approaches to evolve a system and the benefits we get from their use.

The overall goal of this workshop was that of supporting circulation of ideas between these disciplines. Several interactions were expected to take place between reflection, aspect-oriented programming and meta-data for the software evolution, some of which we cannot even foresee. Both the application of reflective or aspect-oriented techniques and concepts to software evolution are likely to support improvement and deeper understanding of these areas. This workshop has represented a good meeting-point for people working in the software evolution area, and an occasion to present reflective, aspect-oriented, and meta-data based solutions to evolutionary problems, and new ideas straddling these areas, to provide a discussion forum, and to allow new collaboration projects to be established. The workshop was a full day meeting. One part of the workshop was devoted to presentation of papers, and another to panels and to the exchange of ideas among participants.

# 2   Workshop Topics and Structure

Every contribution that exploits reflective techniques, aspect-oriented programming and/or meta-data to evolve software systems were welcome. Specific topics of interest for the workshop have included, but were not limited to:

- aspect-oriented middleware and environments for software evolution;
- adaptive software components and evolution as component composition;
- evolution planning and deployment through aspect-oriented techniques and reflective approaches;
- aspect interference and composition for software evolution;
- feature- and subject-oriented adaptation;
- unanticipated software evolution supported by AOSD or reflective techniques;

- MOF, code annotations and other meta-data facilities for software evolution;
- software evolution tangling concerns;
- techniques for refactoring into AOSD and to get the separation of concerns;
- early aspect evolution, i.e., to design evolution by evolving the design information or the application in its early stages of development.

To ensure lively discussion at the workshop, the organizing committee has chosen the contributions on the basis of topic similarity that will permit the beginning of new collaborations. To grant an easy dissemination of the proposed ideas and to favourite an ideas interchange among the participants, accepted contributions are freely downloadable from the workshop web page:

http://homes.dico.unimi.it/RAM-SE08.html

The workshop was a full day meeting organized in three sessions. The morning was devoted to scientific presentations with six refereed papers in the first session and with a keynote speech by hidehiko Masuhara in the second session just before lunch. In the afternoon the workshop became a working group lead by Shigeru Chiba, this has permitted to exchange new ideas in a lively discussion with the several people attending.

The workshop has been very lively, the debates very stimulating, and the high number of participants (see appendix A) testifies the interest in the application of reflective, aspect- and meta-data oriented techniques to software evolution as well as software evolution in general.

## 3   Important References

The following publications are important references for people interested in learning more about the topics of this workshop:

- Pattie Maes. Computational Reflection. PhD thesis, Vrije Universiteit Brussel, Brussels, Belgium, 1987.
- Gregor Kiczales, John Lamping, Anurag Mendhekar, Chris Maeda, Cristina Videira Lopes, Jean-Marc Loingtier, and John Irwin. Aspect-Oriented Programming. In *11th European Conference on Object Oriented Programming (ECOOP'97)*, LNCS 1241, pages 220–242, Helsinki, Finland, June 1997. Springer-Verlag.
- The proceedings of the International Conference on Aspect-Oriented Software Development (AOSD) from 2002 onward. See also http://aosd.net/archive/index.php.
- Several tracks related to aspect-oriented software development and evolution at the International Conference on Software Maintenance (ICSM) and the Working Conference on Reverse Engineering (WCRE), from 2002 onward.
- The software evolution website at the Program Transformation wiki:

http://www.program-transformation.org/twiki/bin/view/
Transform/SoftwareEvolution

- The workshops proceedings of the USE workshop series:

http://www.informatik.uni-bonn.de/~gk/use/

# 4   Workshop Overview: Session by Session

## RAM-SE Paper Presentation

The first morning session focused on presenting accepted papers. The session was moderated by Manuel Oriol.

[1] A Case Study for Aspect Based Updating. *Susanne Cech Previtali* and *Thomas R. Gross* (ETH Zurich, Switzerland).
Susanne Cech Previtali gave the presentation.

[2] Runtime Adaptations within the QuaD$^2$-Framework. *Steffen Mencke, Martin Kunz,* and *Mario Pukall* (Otto von Guericke University Magdeburg, Germany).
Mario Pukall gave the presentation.

[3] Modeling Context-Dependent Aspect Interference Using Default Logics. *Frans Sanen, Eddie Truyen,* and *Wouter Joosen* (K.U. Leuven, Belgium).
Frans Sanen gave the presentation.

[4] Object Roles and Runtime Adaptation in Java. *Mario Pukall* (Otto von Guericke University Magdeburg, Germany).
Mario Pukall gave the presentation.

[5] Exploring Role Based Adaptation. *Sebastian Götz* and *Ilie Savga* (Dresden University of Technology, Germany).
Sebastian Götz gave the presentation.

[6] Annotations for Seamless Aspect Based SW Evolution. *Susanne Cech Previtali* and *Thomas R. Gross* (ETH Zurich, Switzerland).
Susanne Cech Previtali gave the presentation

## Keynote on Toward Right Abstraction of Crosscutting Concerns

In the second session, Hidehiko Masuhara gave a keynote talk moderated by Walter Cazzola:

### Toward Right Abstraction of Crosscutting Concerns.

**Abstract.** *Abstraction mechanisms in programming languages are crucial for modular software development, by drawing a clear boundary among program entities, giving names to those bounded entities, and hiding implementation details. Aspect-oriented programming (AOP) mechanisms can also be viewed as abstraction mechanisms for crosscutting concerns, but differ from traditional ones in what details they hide. In this talk, we discuss the properties of AOP mechanisms that are needed to be right abstraction of crosscutting concerns.*

Matsuhara's presentation gave elements on the definition of crosscutting abstraction as a boundary over the code. The main issue that aspects programmers have to face is that this boundary is actually a very difficult thing to draw precisely. In practice, it is easy to express pointcuts that have a clear mapping into the code, but more complex ones are almost inexpressible.

"Are we Doomed?" as Matsuhara asked. To help defining complex crosscutting concerns it is possible to consider example-based pointcuts. In particular, test-based pointcuts [7] can be of help. The idea is to use unit tests as the main way of defining pointcuts by analysing static execution history. This has several advantages, the main one being that if test cases are maintain, pointcuts should evolve automatically with the application.

The keynote talk fostered further discussions which triggered the following points:

- A boundary might not be the correct abstraction: what space/points can be considered?
- As a lot of people in the workshop saw aspects like a tool for dynamic adaptation, boundaries were usually very easily drawn, but would it be possible to create test-based pointcuts that would draw them?

## RAM-SE'09? Towards the Future

The workshop ended with a session led by Shigeru Chiba on the future of the RAM-SE workshop and fostered lively discussions. Chiba pointed out that dynamic adaptation was one of the main topics this year. It was mostly coded with dynamic aspects and using dynamic aspects to allow adaptation in the future. He also pointed out the fight between statically typed languages and dynamically typed ones and wondered if we are statically typed dynamic languages people. The remaining part of the session was dedicated to how we understand systems that have been adapted over time. Do we need to do aspects refactoring? Should we replace the whole system when adapting it? In the end, are aspects just a tool that enables dynamic refactoring? While discussing all these topics, some pointed out that object-orientation is already aspect-oriented due to multiple dispatch. Aspects are indeed a tool, but they are very good for producing prototypes in a fast and convenient manner.

## 5   Tendencies in Reflection, AOP and Meta-data for Software Evolution

This year, the main area of the workshop was runtime adaptation through aspects. This is a radical shift in the community. It seems that using aspects is nowadays the easiest way to instrument code (at load-time). This meets last year's invited talk presented by Shigeru Chiba that pointed out that logging and transactions were actually the killer-applications for aspects. One more application seems to be the easy instrumentation of code. Because the workshop is targeted at evolution, aspects and reflection, it is thus not too surprising that contributions would focus on it this year.

One of the new adaptation proposed by Cech Previtali and Gross [1] consists in writing updates as an aspect. The paper presents a feasibility study based on the tomcat server and reveals that although all changes cannot be expressed as aspects most of them can. In order to guide the aspect weaver, Cech Previtali and Gross [6] even go as far as to propose annotations in the code so that updates are actually easier to interpret. To achieve a similar goal, Pukall [4] proposes a strategy based on object wrapping and the hotswap technology to change implementation.

Götz and Savga [5] also cope with adapters for objects. They propose a role-based mechanism to manage adapters that would reduce the code complexity.

Another aspect of dynamic adaptation is that adaptation can also be considered not as a timeline punctuated with versions, but rather as a potential for quality of service. Mencke *et al* [2] detail such a system and state that the quality of a combination of a components should govern the choice of components to use.

Sanen *et al* [3] treat a more fundamental question for aspects: how to model aspect interference by using default logic. This would allow developers to use the information when the application evolves.

## 6   Final Remarks

The main goal of the workshop was to bring together researchers interested in the field and have them communicate on their respective work. The workshop lived up to its expectations, with high-quality submissions and presentations, and lively and stimulating discussions. The vitality of the work as well as the lively discussions that took place during the workshop show that the issues addressed by the workshop are plainly relevant and need such a forum to be discussed. We hope participants found the workshop interesting and useful, and encourage them to finalize their position papers and submit them as full papers to international conferences interested in the topics of this workshop.

**Acknowledgements.** We wish to thank all the researchers that have participated to the workshop.

We have also to thank the Department of Informatics and Communication of the University of Milan, the Department of Mathematical and Computing Sciences of the Tokyo institute of Technology, ETH Zurich and the Institute für Technische und Betriebliche Informationssysteme, Otto-von-Guericke-Universität Magdeburg for their various supports.

## References

1. Cech Previtali, S., Gross, T.: A case study for aspect based updating. In: Cazzola, W., Chiba, S., Coady, Y., Oriol, M. (eds.) Proceedings of ECOOP 2008 Workshop on Reflection, AOP and Meta-Data for Software Evolution (RAM-SE 2008), Paphos, Cyprus (2008)

2. Mencke, S., Kunz, M., Pukall, M.: Runtime adaptations within the QuaD$^2$-framework. In: Cazzola, W., Chiba, S., Coady, Y., Oriol, M. (eds.) Proceedings of ECOOP 2008 Workshop on Reflection, AOP and Meta-Data for Software Evolution (RAM-SE 2008), Paphos, Cyprus (2008)
3. Sanen, F., Truyen, E., Joosen, W.: Modeling context-dependent aspect interference using default logics. In: Cazzola, W., Chiba, S., Coady, Y., Oriol, M. (eds.) Proceedings of ECOOP 2008 Workshop on Reflection, AOP and Meta-Data for Software Evolution (RAM-SE 2008), Paphos, Cyprus (2008)
4. Pukall, M.: Object roles and runtime adaptation in java. In: Cazzola, W., Chiba, S., Coady, Y., Oriol, M. (eds.) Proceedings of ECOOP 2008 Workshop on Reflection, AOP and Meta-Data for Software Evolution (RAM-SE 2008), Paphos, Cyprus (2008)
5. Götz, S., Savga, I.: Oexploring role based adaptation. In: Cazzola, W., Chiba, S., Coady, Y., Oriol, M. (eds.) Proceedings of ECOOP 2008 Workshop on Reflection, AOP and Meta-Data for Software Evolution (RAM-SE 2008), Paphos, Cyprus (2008)
6. Cech Previtali, S., Gross, T.: Annotations for seamless aspect based software evolution. In: Cazzola, W., Chiba, S., Coady, Y., Oriol, M. (eds.) Proceedings of ECOOP 2008 Workshop on Reflection, AOP and Meta-Data for Software Evolution (RAM-SE 2008), Paphos, Cyprus (2008)
7. Sakurai, K., Masuhara, H.: Test-based pointcuts for robust and fine-grained join point specification. In: D'Hondt, T. (ed.) AOSD, pp. 96–107. ACM, New York (2008)

# A    Workshop Attendee

The success of the workshop is mainly due to the people that have attended it and to their effort to participate to the discussions. The following is the list of the attendees in alphabetical order.

| Name | Affiliation | Country | e-mail |
|---|---|---|---|
| Arcelli, Francesca | University of Milano Bicocca | Italy | arcelli@disco.unimib.it |
| Bierman, Gavin | Microsoft Research | The Netherlands | gmb@microsoft.com |
| Cazzola, Walter | Università degli Studi di Milano | Italy | cazzola@dico.unimi.it |
| Cech Previtali, Susanne | ETH Zürich | Switzerland | scech@inf.ethz.ch |
| Chiba, Shigeru | Tokyo Institute of Technology | Japan | chiba@is.titech.ac.jp |
| de Roo, Arjan | University of Twente | The Netherlands | a.j.deroo@ewi.utwente.nl |
| Figueiredo, Eduardo | Lancaster University | UK | e.figueiredo@lancaster.ac.uk |
| Götz, Sebastian | Technical University of Dresden | Germany | sebastian.goetz@mail.inf.tu-dresden.de |
| Guerra, Eduardo | ITA - Brazil | Brazil | guerra@ita.br |
| Havinga, Wilke | University of Twente | The Netherlands | havingaw@ewi.utwente.nl |
| Herrmann, Stephan | Technical University of Berlin | Germany | stephan@cs.tu-berlin.de |
| Kakousis, Constantinos | University of Cyprus | Cyprus | kakousis@os.ucy.ac.cy |
| Masuhara, Hidehiko | University of Tokyo | Japan | masuhara@graco.c.u-tokyo.ac.jp |
| Oriol, Manuel | ETH Zürich | Switzerland | moriol@inf.ethz.ch |
| Ostrowski, Krzystof | Cornell University | USA | krzys@cs.cornell.edu |
| Pukall, Mario | University of Magdeburg | Germany | pukall@iti.cs.uni-magdeburg.de |
| Sanen, Frans | KULeuven | Belgium | frans.sanen@cs.kuleuven.be |
| Vandemonde, Yves | KULeuven | Belgium | yves.vandemonde@cs.kuleuven.be |

# Formal Techniques for Java-Like Programs
## Report on the 10th Workshop FTfJP at ECOOP 2008

Elvira Albert[1], Anindya Banerjee[2], Sophia Drossopoulou[3],
Marieke Huisman[4,*], Atsushi Igarashi[5], Gary T. Leavens[6],
Peter Müller[7], and Tobias Wrigstad[8]

[1] Complutense University of Madrid, Spain
[2] Kansas State University, USA
[3] Imperial College London, UK
[4] University of Twente, Netherlands
[5] Kyoto University, Japan
[6] University of Central Florida, USA
[7] ETH Zurich, Switzerland
[8] Purdue University, USA

**Abstract.** This report gives an overview of the 10th Workshop on Formal Techniques for Java-like Programs at ECOOP 2008. It explains the motivation for the workshop, and summarizes the presentations and discussions.

## 1 Introduction

Formal techniques can help analyze programs, precisely describe program behavior, and verify program properties. Newer languages such as Java and C# provide good platforms to bridge the gap between formal techniques and practical program development, because of their reasonably clear semantics and standardized libraries. Moreover, these languages are interesting targets for formal techniques, because the novel paradigm for program deployment introduced with Java, with its improved portability and mobility, opens up new possibilities for abuse and causes concern about security.

Work on formal techniques and tools for programs and work on the formal underpinnings of programming languages themselves naturally complement each other. This workshop aims to bring together people working in both these fields, on topics such as: program verification, formal models and extensions of Java-like languages, program analysis, and type systems.

The workshop was organized by Marieke Huisman (INRIA Sophia Antipolis, France), Sophia Drossopoulou (Imperial College London, UK), Susan Eisenbach (Imperial College London, UK), Gary T. Leavens (University of Central Florida, USA), Peter Müller (Microsoft Research, Redmond, USA), Arnd Poetzsch-Heffter (University of Kaiserslautern, Germany), and Erik Poll (Radboud University Nijmegen, Netherlands). The selection of papers was done by a larger program

---

* Affiliated with INRIA Sophia Antipolis at the time of the workshop.

P. Eugster (Ed.): ECOOP 2008 Workshop Reader, LNCS 5475, pp. 70–76, 2009.

committee chaired by Marieke Huisman. The committee members are listed at the end of this report.

Around 40 people attended this full-day workshop. A representative list of participants is given at the end of this report. A number of other participants dropped by for specific presentations, to chat with particular speakers, etc. To encourage cross-fertilization with related research areas, the IWACO and FTfJP workshops organized a joint workshop dinner.

**Overview of the presented papers.** Sixteen research papers were submitted, of which eleven were accepted for presentation at the workshop. The program committee made its selection after a fruitful discussion. Besides quality of the submission, also potential interest of the presentation for the workshop participants was used as a criterion.

The accepted papers are collected in informal proceedings that are available as technical report ICIS-R08013 from the Radboud University Nijmegen, Netherlands, available at http://www.cs.ru.nl/~erikpoll/ftfjp/FTfJP08

The topics addressed by the presented papers are:

– program verification;
– formal models and extensions for Java-like languages;
– program analysis; and
– type systems.

For each topic, the sections below briefly describe the presentations and discussions.

## 2   Program Verification

Jan Smans talked about joint research with Bart Jacobs and Frank Piessens on the verification of implicit dynamic frames. Dynamic frames are a powerful mechanism for modular verification. They propose a technique that avoids the need to explicitly specify and verify frame conditions; these are replaced by accessibility predicates from which an upper bound on the set of locations that may be modified can be inferred. The technique has been implemented in a tool set, and Jan demonstrated how it could be used to verify several challenging examples. The discussion following the presentation revolved around the similarities with Banerjee et al.'s work on regional logic which was to be presented in the following days as a part of ECOOP's technical track. In regional logic, region expressions can be used to explicitly specify read and write effects that, similar to dynamic frames, needs to be checked at verification time. Implicit dynamic frames do not require these explicit annotations but rely on inferring frame information from preconditions. Finally, the discussion also touched briefly on the subject of patterns, in particular the application to examples involving more layers of structure, e.g. the Composite pattern, which would be useful to test the practical usability of the proposed tool set. However, this did not arrive at any conclusion.

Romain Bardou presented a way to reason about pointer arithmetic and memory separation for low-level languages, based on ownership systems. Because of the low-level language features that are supported by his approach, the verification technique can be applied to C programs. In the following discussion, Dino DiStefano and others questioned whether the assumption of fresh pointer locations was sound in the presence of pointers and pointer arithmetic and that in a C program, a newly allocated object may be given an address already pointed to by preexisting variables. Currently, Bardou's simple formalisation does not model memory deallocation.

The last talk in this session was given by Dave Cunningham, who presented joint work with Susan Eisenbach and Sophia Drossopoulou on the formalization of a lock inference algorithm. A good way to structure concurrent programs (and thus make them less error-prone) is the use of atomic sections. This is a high-level primitive, which can be compiled into transactional memory accesses or a locking schema. This paper discusses an efficient and precise algorithm that infers locks from atomic sections. The algorithm is formalized in Isabelle/HOL and proven correct. The discussion evolved around the possibility to combine lock inference with partial program annotations.

# 3   Formal Models and Extensions of Java-Like Languages

John Boyland presented a new style operational semantics for a concurrent language with fork-join parallelism, synchronization, and volatile fields. The operational semantics introduces the notion of "write-key", which simulates the happens before order of relaxed memory models, i.e., it indicates whether a certain write could happen based on what happened before in the program. The paper then shows that exhibiting a write-key error in the operational semantics is equivalent to the program containing a data race. The advantage of this approach is that write-key errors can be detected locally, whereas data races cannot. The operational semantics and equivalence proof are formalized using Twelf. The discussion mainly focused on issues about the correctness results. There was one question which clarified that correctness holds for any possible execution and not only for a given entry. Also, another question made clear that there is no order required on the write-keys and neither are time-stamps.

Next, Gabriele Costa proposed an extension of Java's security model that would allow to specify, analyze, and enforce history-based security policies. This is joint work with Massimo Bartoletti, Pierpaolo Degano, Fabio Martinelli, and Roberto Zunino. Crucial to the approach is that the policies are local, which makes them easier to enforce and allows for safe composition of programs and their security requirements. This paper designs a run-time mechanism for the enforcement of local history-based security properties, and then further optimizes this, based on a static analysis that detects when a policy might be violated—and thus allows one to discard checks that never fail. During the discussion, Gabriele explained that the models which are obtained for the policies are finite with respect to the number of states. He also clarified that the expressiveness of their approach is comparable to other history-based approaches.

The last paper in this session was presented by Tetsuo Kamina. He discussed joint work with Tetuso Tamai on a small core language that formalizes key concepts of object adaptability, i.e., the ability of an object to change its behavior dynamically. The small core language is compared with the earlier proposed Epsilon model for object adaptability, and it turns out to be an appropriate formal base for this model .After the presentation, there were several suggestions to improve this work by various workshop participants. One comment was how to handle multiplicity by giving rules for valid multiplicity such that if they are violated then the program is not valid. Another suggestion was to use a typed execution model. Further the relation of this work with roles was discussed, and also, how one could handle the situation where a role defined in a subclass imposes constraints on roles as inherited from superclasses.

## 4  Program Analysis

The next session started with Elvira Albert presenting joint work with Puri Arenas, Samir Genaim, and Germán Puebla on the handling of numeric fields to automatically prove termination of programs written in a Java-like language. Statistics have revealed that in the Java libraries for over 10% of the loops, termination depends on the values stored in numeric fields. The presentation gave an overview of different program patterns where termination depends on numeric fields, and it sketched how termination proofs for these programs could be found automatically. The discussion evolved on the precision of the analysis, the merits of performing analysis at byte-code or source code level, and a comparison with any optimizations performed by the Java compiler, in particular whether the transformation of field accesses to local variables is already done by the Java compiler.

Next, Rok Strniša presented his work on the Java module system. He analyzed and formalised the core of two JSRs that propose a new module system for Java (which will be part of Java 7). The analysis revealed several shortcomings in the proposal, w.r.t. module instantiations and class resolution. The presentation further proposed clean solutions to these problems, that are also modeled formally (using Isabelle/HOL). This allowed him to prove type soundness for the corrected version of the module system. The discussion evolved on the modifications to the module system suggested by Rok, the practical ramifications of the proposed solutions, and in particular in how far these modifications would be agreeable to the Java community. We also discussed the role of the formal model in discovering these shortcomings.

Last, Samir Genaim presented joint work with Fausto Spoto on the detection of purity of method arguments, by means of an abstract domain where "constancy" is defined as an abstract interpretation. The presentation concluded with examples of how constancy information can be used to improve the precision of other, existing static analyses. The discussion centered around the comparison of static analyses based on constancy with effect systems based approaches to constancy.

## 5   Types

The last session started with Alexander Summers presenting joint work with Sophia Drossopoulou and Peter Müller on a Universe-Type based verification technique for static fields and methods. In particular, he discussed how the use of Universe Types for the verification of invariants should be adapted for a language that contains static fields and methods. This required to extend Universe Type hierarchy such that each ownership tree is rooted in a class. This allows classes to own object instances as their static fields. Furthermore, methods need to be annotated by the classes whose static methods they may (directly or indirectly) invoke. These annotations can be reduced by organizing classes in layers. The presentation was followed by a discussion of whether the approach can be made more lightweight by inferring the levels of classes, and the annotations. Also, there was a question whether partial, instead of linear, orders could be used for the partitions of classes; the authors conjectured partial orders could be used.

The last presentation of the workshop was given by Stefan Wehr, who presented joint work with Peter Thieman on subtyping existential types. Existential types are often advocated as a powerful feature that can subsume Java's interface and wildcard types, and several proposals exist to extend Java-like languages with existential types. However, Stefan showed that existential types do not mingle well with subtyping, and make type checking undecidable. He concluded with some possible compromises that allow most of the features of existential types, but keep the subtyping relation decidable. The following discussion centered on the implication of the work on decidability for Java wildcards, and newer applications of existential types into ownership types.

## 6   Conclusions

A special issue for FTfJP 2008 will appear in the Journal of Object Technology (JOT).

This was the tenth workshop in the series, and the workshop is still going strong. The focus of the workshop has shifted somewhat over time, as different topics become more or less popular, or essentially resolved, while others have gained importance. Moreover, the revival of IWACO (International Workshop on Aliasing, Confinement and Ownership in object-oriented programming) has also contributed to this shift. It is nice to observe that the workshop has helped in raising some interesting topics for research, and to observe the way it has contributed to fostering collaborations, all of which has resulted in good work presented not just at this workshop but also at the main ECOOP conference.

The workshop has somewhat outgrown the standard workshop format, given the number and quality of submissions it typically received, and the number of people that want to participate. But the interest it generates and the audience it attracts proves that it clearly serves a useful purpose and we look forward to organizing another FTfJP workshop at next year's ECOOP.

## Program Committee

Elvira Albert, Complutense University of Madrid (Spain)
Cyrille Artho, RCIS/AIST (Japan)
Anindya Banerjee, Kansas State University (USA)
Mike Barnett, Microsoft Research, Redmond (USA)
Amy Felty, University of Ottawa (Canada)
Paola Giannini, University of Eastern Piedmont (Italy)
Rene Rydhof Hansen, Aalborg University (Denmark)
Marieke Huisman (chair), INRIA Sophia Antipolis (France)
Atsushi Igarashi, Kyoto University (Japan)
Bart Jacobs, University of Leuven (Belgium)
Gerwin Klein, National ICT Australia (Australia)
Neelakantan R. Krishnaswami, Carnegie Mellon University (USA)
Matthew Parkinson, University of Cambridge (UK)
Arnd Poetzsch-Heffter, University of Kaiserslautern (Germany)
Tobias Wrigstad, Purdue University (USA)

## List of Participants

Suad Alagic, University of Southern Maine (USA)
Elvira Albert, Complutense University of Madrid (Spain)
Jonathan Aldrich, Carnegie Mellon University (USA)
Anindya Banerjee, Kansas State University (USA)
Romain Bardou, INRIA Saclay (France)
Massimo Bartoletti, Universitá di Pisa (Italy)
Frederic Besson, IRISA/INRIA (France)
John Boyland, University of Wisconsin-Milwaukee (USA)
Nicholas Cameron, Imperial College (UK)
Dave Clarke, CWI (The Netherlands)
David Cunningham, Imperial College (UK)
Dino Distefano, University of Cambridge (UK)
Sophia Drossopoulou, Imperial College (UK)
Patrick Eugster, Purdue University (USA)
Adrian Fiech, Memorial University (Canada)
Samir Genaim, Technical University of Madrid (Spain)
Paola Gianini, Alessandria (Italy)
Christian Haack, Radboud University Nijmegen (The Netherlands)
Clement Hurlin, INRIA (France)
Atsushi Igarashi, Kyoto University (Japan)
Tetsuo Kamina, The University of Tokyo (Japan)
Gary T. Leavens, University of Central Florida (USA)
Yu David Liu, The Johns Hopkins University (USA)
Nicholas Matsakis, ETH Zurich (Switzerland)
Ana Milanova, Rensselaer Polytechnic Institute (USA)

Peter Müller, Microsoft Research (USA)
James Noble, Victoria University of Wellington (New Zealand)
Johan Oetlund, Purdue University (USA)
Alex Potanin, Victoria University of Wellington (New Zealand)
Germán Puebla, Technical University of Madrid (Spain)
Jan Smans, Katholieke Universiteit Leuven (Belgium)
Rok Strniša, University of Cambridge (UK)
Alex Summers, Imperial College (UK)
Tiphaine Turpin, IRISA/INRIA (France)
Jan Vitek, Purdue University (USA)
Stefan Wehr, University of Freiburg (Germany)
Tobias Wrigstad, Purdue University (USA)

# Quantitative Approaches in Object-Oriented Software Engineering
## Report on the 12th Workshop QAOOSE at ECOOP 2008

Giovanni Falcone[1], Yann-Gaël Guéhéneuc[2], Christian F.J. Lange[3],
Zoltán Porkoláb[4], and Houari Sahraoui[1]

[1] Lehrstuhl für Softwaretechnik,
Universität Mannheim, Germany
[2] Department of Computer Science and Operations Research,
Université Montréal, Canada
[3] Software Engineering and Technology Group,
Eindhoven University of Technology, The Netherlands
[4] Department of Programming Languages and Compilers,
Eötvös Loránd University, Hungary

**Abstract.** The QAOOSE 2008 workshop has been held at ECOOP 2008 conference in Paphos, Cyprus on July 8th, 2008. This was the twelfth of the series of QAOOSE workshops intended to bring researchers and practitioners both from academia and industry together. The workshop provided a forum to discuss the current state of the art and the practice in the area of quantitative approaches in the fields related to object-orientation. This report includes a summary of the technical presentations and the subsequent discussions. Six papers has been accepted by the workshop organizers. The presentations were followed by vivid discussions.

## 1   Introduction

QAOOSE 2008 is a direct continuation of eleven successful workshops, held during previous editions of ECOOP in Berlin (2008), Nantes (2006), Glasgow (2005), Oslo (2004), Darmstadt (2003), Malaga (2002), Budapest (2001), Cannes (2000), Lisbon (1999), Brussels (1998) and Aarhus (1995). The QAOOSE series of workshops has attracted participants from both academia and industry that are involved/interested in the application of quantitative methods in object-oriented software engineering research and practice. Quantitative approaches in the object-oriented field are a broad and active research areas that develop and/or evaluate methods, practical guidelines, techniques, and tools to improve the quality of software products and the efficiency and effectiveness of software processes. The workshop is open to other technologies related to object-oriented such as component-based systems, web-based systems, and agent-based systems.

This workshop provides a forum to discuss the current state of the art and the practice in the area of quantitative approaches in the fields related to object-orientation. A blend of researchers and practitioners from industry and academia

P. Eugster (Ed.): ECOOP 2008 Workshop Reader, LNCS 5475, pp. 77–86, 2009.
© Springer-Verlag Berlin Heidelberg 2009

is expected to share recent advances in the field success or failure stories, lessons learned, and seek to identify new fundamental problems arising in the field.

## 2    The Workshop Program

| 09:00 - 09:15 | Welcome and QAOOSE introduction |
|---|---|
| 09:15 - 10:30 | Session 1: Graph-based Assessment |
| 09:15 - 09:45 | Quantitative Comparison of MC/DC and DC Test Methods<br>Zalán Szűgyi and Zoltán Porkoláb |
| 09:45 - 10:15 | The AV-graph in SQL-Based Environment<br>Norbert Pataki, Melinda Simon, and Zoltn Porkolb |
| 10:15 - 10:30 | Session Discussion |
| 10:30 - 10:45 | Session Break |
| 10:30 - 11:45 | Session 2: Quality Assessment |
| 10:30 - 11:00 | Quantitative analysis of testability antipatterns on open source Java applications<br>Muhammad Rabee Shaheen and Lydie du Bousquet |
| 11:00 - 11:30 | Evaluating Quality-in-Use Using Bayesian Networks<br>M.A Moraga, M.F. Bertoa, M.C. Morcillo, C. Calero, A. Vallecillo |
| 11:30 - 11:45 | Session Discussion |
| 11:45 - 12:15 | Coffee Break |
| 12:15 - 13:30 | Session 3: Metrics |
| 12:15 - 12:45 | Metrics for Analyzing the Quality of Model Transformations<br>M.F. van Amstel, C.F.J. Lange, and M.G.J. van den Brand |
| 12:45 - 13:15 | A Basis for a Metric Suite for Software Components<br>Giovanni Falcone and Colin Atkinson |
| 13:15 - 13:30 | Session Discussion |
| 13:30 - 15:30 | Lunch Break |
| 15:30 - 17:00 | Session 4<br>Discussions and/or Work on a common problem/project/paper |

## 3    Presentations

### 3.1    Quantitative Comparison of MC/DC and DC Test Methods

Zalán Szűgyi and Zoltán Porkoláb
Department of Programming Languages and Compilers,
Eötvös Loránd University
Pázmány Péter sétány 1/C H-1117 Budapest, Hungary
{lupin, gsd}@elte.hu

Coverage refers to the extent to which a given verification activity has satisfied its objectives. There are several types of coverage analysis exists to check the code correctness. Usually the less strict analysis methods require fewer test cases to satisfy their requirements and the more strict ones require more. But it is not clear how much is the "more". In this paper we concern to the Decision Coverage and the more strict Modified Condition / Decision Coverage [1]. The authors examined several projects used in the industry by several aspects: McCabe metric, nesting and maximal argument number in decisions. The paper discusses how these aspects are affected the difference of the necessary test cases for these testing methods.

The authors analyzed several projects written in Ada programming language and estimated the difference of the required test cases of Decision Coverage and the more strict Modified Condition / Decision Coverage [2]. They found that the difference is about five to ten per cent because the decisions in most subprograms have only one argument and there are several subprograms which do not contain decisions at all. If we exclude these subprograms we get a difference that is four times larger. Most importantly, the maximum number of arguments in decisions affects the difference. For those subprograms where there are decisions with more than six arguments, almost twice as many MC/DC test cases are needed as DC. But these subprograms are only less than one per cent of the whole project. The authors' intention for future work is to refine the analyzer program to do a better estimation in some exceptional cases, and they plan to do this analysis for some open source and other industrial projects too.

## 3.2   The AV-Graph in SQL-Based Environment

Norbert Pataki, Melinda Simon, and Zoltán Porkoláb
Department of Programming Languages and Compilers,
Eötvös Loránd University
Pázmány Péter sétány 1/C H-1117 Budapest, Hungary
{patakino, melinda, gsd}@elte.hu

Multiparadigm metrics can be used in various situations for various purposes. This paper presents a description of the problem of a multi-paradigm environment and argues that the measurement of multiparadigm programs need to be done using multparadigm metrics. SQL (Structured Query Language) is the most common language defining and manipulating data in databases [3]. However, SQL is not an imperative language but a declarative one. In this paper the authors analize the behaviour of AV-graph, a multiparadigm software metrics [4] that also can be used in SQL supported environment.

The paper informally introduces AV-graph and describes the meaning of AV-graph in the SQL language. They extend the AV-graph metric to languages supporting embedded SQL. The authors specificate the connection between the metric and language in a sophisticated way and give some examples to check it on real queries. Some open problems are defined too. Unfortunately, the paper does not include any measurement for real-world artifacts yet, developing such tools is the future plan of the authors.

### 3.3 Quantitative Analysis of Testability Antipatterns on Open Source Java Applications

Muhammad Rabee Shaheen and Lydie du Bousquet
Laboratoire Informatique de Grenoble (LIG)
Universites de Grenoble (UJF)
B.P. 72 - F-38402 - Saint Martin dHéres Cedex - France
{muhammad-rabee.shaheen,lydie.du-bousquet}@imag.fr

Testability is a software characteristic that aims at producing systems easy to test. Antipatterns is a factor that could affect negatively the testability of a software. Dependency is the main idea that is found behind different studies related to antipatterns. Testability antipatterns identify the existed weaknesses in a design pattern. In this paper the authors introduce a quantitative analysis to show some factors that lead to increase the antipatterns [5].

Testability is a software factor that could be used to detect the different weaknesses that could increase the difficulty of the test. Several metrics have been proposed to evaluate the testability of object oriented programs [6]. Certain metrics were defined at representation facet other were defined at implementation facet. Antipatterns are weaknesses that reduce the testability of a software. The antipatterns could be detected early in the life cycle of software development. The goal of the authors' quantitative analysis was to find if there is any relationship between the occurrence of antipatterns and the characteristics of the code.

This study is based on 14 open-source Java applications. The results presented here show that about 50% of cycles are of size 2, and 20% of cycles are of size 3. On the other hand the analysis showed that 56.48% of classes that belong to cycles are inner classes. As a result about 70% of cycles could be avoided if one limits the use of cycles of size 2 and 3. And one can reduce the size of the cycles by avoiding the number of inner classes that present more than 55%.

For the future work, authors are looking for other structural elements that could increase the occurrence of the cycles i.e. inheritance, complexity.

### 3.4 Evaluating Quality-in-Use Using Bayesian Networks

M.A Moraga, M.F. Bertoa, M.C. Morcillo, C. Calero1, A. Vallecillo
Alarcos Research Group  Institute of Information Technologies & Systems
Dept. Information Technologies & Systems  Escuela Superior de Informtica
Universidad de Castilla-La Mancha, Spain
Dept. Lenguajes y Ciencias de la Computación
Universidad de Málaga, Spain
Dept. Estadística e Investigación Operativa.
Universidad de Málaga, Spain

This paper challenges the traditional approach for assessing the overall quality of a software product, which is based on the assumption that, in ISO/IEC 9126 terms, a good external quality ensures a good quality-in-use. Here the authors change the focus of the quality assessment, concentrating on the quality-in-use as the driving factor for designing a software product, or for selecting the product that better fits a user's need. The authors propose a "backwards" analysis of the relationship between the external quality and the quality-in-use which tries to determine the external quality sub-characteristics that are really relevant to ensure the required level of quality in a given context of use, in order to avoid superfluous costs or irrelevant features – which may unnecessarily increase the final price of the product [7,8].

In this paper Bayesian Belief Networks is used to model such relationships, and propose a method to build them for different contexts of use. It has been shown how to build a BN for determining the influence of EQ sub-characteristics on the overall QiU of a software product. Fenton et al. [9] have also used BNs to predict some EQ characteristics from the internal quality of software products, but without considering the QiU, and using a "forward" prediction process. The authors' aim is, however, to focus on the QiU and use a backwards analysis for predicting the minimum acceptance levels for EQ characteristics that ensure the required QiU.

Of course, this is just the first step of a more complete line of work that aims at providing users of given contexts of use with tool support for evaluating software products (including, e.g., the selection of those products that better suit their needs with the less possible costs).

There are several activities that the authors plan to address in the short term. Firstly, they want to empirically validate the proposal by exercising the BN in several contexts of use, adapting the BN to the specific peculiarities of each context, and checking that it learns as it should for these contexts. The final results of these tests will be a set of trained BNs that we expect to be useful in these environments. The way to validate the results (conducting some experimental validation exercises) is a research activity itself.

Secondly, the authors also want to refine this approach by combining it with some Principal Component Analysis during the initial definition of the BN, whereby they can confirm (and refine) the relationships between the EQ subcharacteristics and the QiU characteristics. Finally, they expect to provide a useful input to the ISO Working Group defining the new SQUARE family of standards based on their researches, not only confirming the existence of the influence of EQ on QiU, but also quantifying it in some specific contexts of use; and, more importantly, highlighting the primary role that QiU plays in the evaluation of the quality of any software product as the driving force of the rest of the quality views.

## 3.5   Metrics for Analyzing the Quality of Model Transformations

M.F. van Amstel1, C.F.J. Lange2, M.G.J. van den Brand
Department of Mathematics and Computer Science
Eindhoven University of Technology
Den Dolech 2, P.O. Box 513, 5600 MB Eindhoven, The Netherlands
{M.F.v.Amstel,M.G.J.v.d.Brand}@tue.nl

Federal Office for Information Technology
Barbarastrae 1, 50735 Cologne, Germany
mail@christian-lange.com

Model transformations become increasingly important with the emergence of model driven engineering of, amongst others, object-oriented software systems. It is therefore necessary to define and evaluate the quality of model transformations. The goal of this research is to make the quality of model transformations measurable. This position paper presents the first results of this ongoing research. It presents the quality attributes the authors have identified thus far and a set of metrics to assess these quality attributes.

The main contribution is a set of eight quality attributes that can be used to assess the quality of model transformations. To refine these quality attributes and make them tangible, the authors have presented a set of metrics that can be used to assess these quality attributes. The initial results are presented in this position paper are a basis for future work in the direction of quality of model transformations. To assess the quality of model transformations, a clear definition of quality is needed first. The authors presented the eight quality attributes they identified thus far. They plan to extend this set of quality attributes and relate them in a quality model such as proposed in [10]. In this paper they focused on ASF+SDF model transformations. They expect that our techniques can be generalized and applied to other model transformation formalisms, such as ATL as well. The intended quality model will be the same, but some metrics to assess the quality attributes need to be adapted to the specifics of the transformation formalism. Authors proposed the metric number of functions as a measure for the size of a transformation created in ASF+SDF. For model transformations created with ATL the number of transformation rules could be used to measure size. However, they expect that most metrics will be conceptually the same for different transformation formalisms. They want to verify their approach by means of empirical case studies. It is infeasible and inaccurate to extract metrics from model transformations by hand. Therefore they have to implement a tool that can automatically extract the values of all of the metrics from a model transformation. Furthermore visualisation of the values of metrics in such a way that outliers and striking values can easily be observed. Something similar has been done for software designs [11].

Once the authors have identified quality problems in model transformations, they can propose a methodology for improving their quality. This methodology will probably consist of a set of guidelines which, if adhered to, lead to high-quality model transformations.

### 3.6  A Basis for a Metric Suite for Software Components

Giovanni Falcone and Colin Atkinson
Chair of Softwareengineering, University of Mannheim, Germany
{gfalcone,atkinson}@informatik.uni-mannheim.de

Although software components have been used in software engineering for quite some time, only a small number of metric suites have been designed to capture the idiosyncrasies of components and the systems developed from them [12]. Moreover, these are rather limited because they treat components as if they were objects in an object-oriented programming language. In this paper the authors outline a more component-oriented metric suite which is based on four distinct views of components – external, shallow, deep and complete. By measuring the various properties of a component from these different viewpoints it is possible to create metrics which capture the relative distribution of "realization" between the component's own application logic, its nested components and its external used components. These, in turn, are likely to be indicators of quality characteristics such as reliability and maintainability.

In the paper the authors presented the idea behind a novel a metric suite which is customized for software components. They have identified four fundamental views of components and used these to define a range of different metrics based on the core structural and architectural properties of components. The two final relative metrics in the previous are two of the most interesting from their point of view since they will be strong indicators of important external characteristics of a component. For example, authors suspect that the Proportion External Cyclomatic Complexity (PECC) will be a good indicator of likely dependability since it is the use of external functionality in component and service based architecture which bears the highest risk. Similarly, authors believe that the Proportion Delegated Cyclomatic Complexity (PDCC) will be a good indicator of the maintainability of a component because it indicates how much of functionality of the component needs to be maintained and how much is obtained from used components.

Although the deep and complete metrics theoretically include information about the nested and external components, the authors do not want to have to examine them in detail to calculate the deep and complete metrics. Rather the goal is to be able to calculate the deep and complete metrics for a component using the corresponding shallow and deep metrics for its sub and external components. This should be possible because with one exception the metrics would appear to be additive. The one exception is when a component that is external to a subcomponent is not external to its super component. The authors are currently working on a strategy to address this issue. They also plan to focus their investigation on how these metrics relate to quality characteristics like effort, reliability, maintainability, etc. Additionally they plan to analyze how these metrics relate to other metrics suites like the OO metrics.

## 4   The Organizers

**Giovanni Falcone**
University of Mannheim, Germany
falcone@informatik.uni-mannheim.de

Giovanni Falcone is a PhD student at the Chair of Software Engineering, University of Mannheim, Germany. His PhD has the working title "A metric suite for hierarchical component based systems" and will be completed in 2009. His research interests include high performance computing, hardware/software codesign, model driven architecture, object-oriented metrics, metrics for component based systems, and software quality.

**Yann-Gaël Guéhéneuc**
University of Montreal, Canada
guehene@iro.umontreal.ca

Yann-Gaël Guéhéneuc is assistant professor at the Department of Informatics and Operations Research (Software Engineering Group) of University of Montreal. He holds a Ph.D. in software engineering from University of Nantes, France (under Professor Pierre Cointe's supervision) since 2003 and an Engineering Diploma from cole des Mines of Nantes since 1998. His PhD thesis was funded by Object Technology International, Inc. (now IBM OTI Labs.), where he worked in 1999 and 2000. His research interests are program understanding and program quality during development and maintenance, in particular through reverse engineering and the identification of recurring patterns. He is also interested in empirical software engineering and in software laws and theories. He has published many papers in international conferences and leads the Ptidej team, which develops a tool suite to evaluate and to enhance the quality of object-oriented programs by promoting the use of patterns.

**Christian Lange**
Eindhoven, University of Technology, The Netherlands
mail@christian-lange.com

Christian Lange is a postdoctoral researcher in the Software Engineering and Technology Group at the Eindhoven University of Technology (The Netherlands). In 2007 he finished his PhD titled "Assessing and Improving the Quality of Modeling: A Series of Empirical Studies about the UML". His research interests include empirical software engineering, quantitative approaches, software quality, program comprehension, software architecture and software evolution. He is the initiator of the EmpAnADa project for Empirical Analysis of Architecture and Design Quality at the TU Eindhoven. He is also the initiator of the MetricView tool. Christian Lange has published more than 20 papers in international journals, conferences, and workshops such as: IEEE Software, ICSE, MoDELS/UML, ICPC, HICSS, or QAOOSE. He has served in the organizing committee of several international workshops, such as QAOOSE, Model Size Metrics (MSM, co-located with MODELS, and the BENEVOL workshop for research on software evolution in Belgium and the Netherlands.

**Zoltán Porkoláb**
Eötvös Loránd University, Hungary
gsd@elte.hu

Zoltán Porkoláb is associate professor at the Department of Programming Languages and Compilers, at the Faculty of Informatics, Eötvös Loránd University,

Budapest, Hungary, with almost 20 years of teaching experience both in the higher education and in the form of industrial trainings. He has finished his PhD in 2003 on the structured complexity of object-oriented programs. His research area is generative programming and software complexity, especially the connections between metrics and software paradigms. He has published more than 60 papers in journals, conferences, and workshops. He has served in organizing committees, such ECOOP 2001, and programming committees, like GPCE 2007. He is the main organizer of WGT, an ETAPS satellite workshop series.

**Houari A. Sahraoui**
University of Montreal, Canada
sahraouh@iro.umontreal.ca

Houari A. Sahraoui is associate professor at the Department of Computer Science and Operations Research (Software Engineering Group) of University of Montreal. Before joining the university, he held the position of lead researcher of the software engineering group at CRIM (research center on computer science, Montreal). He holds an Engineering Diploma from the National Institute of Computer Science (1990), Algiers, and a Ph.D. in Computer Science, Pierre and Marie Curie University LIP6, Paris, 1995. His research interests include the application of artificial intelligence techniques to software engineering, object-oriented metrics, software quality, software visualization, and software reverse- and re-engineering. He has published around 100 papers in conferences, workshops, and journals and edited two books. He served as steering, program and organization committee member in several major conferences (ECOOP, ASE, METRICS, ICSM...) and as member of the editorial boards of two journals. He was the general chair of the IEEE Automated Software Engineering Conference in 2003.

# References

1. Hayhurst, K.J., Veerhusen, D.S.: A Practical Approach to Modified Condition/Decision Coverage. In: 20th Digital Avionics Systems Conference (DASC), Daytona Beach, Florida, USA, October 14-18, 2001, vol. 1, pp. 1B2/1-1B2/10 (2001)
2. Szűgyi, Z., Porkoláb, Z.: Necessary test cases for Decision Coverage and Modified Condition / Decision Coverage. In: Proceedings of 6th CSCS Conference, July 2-5 (2008)
3. van den Brink, H., van der Leek, R., Visser, J.: Quality Assesment for Embedded SQL. In: Proc. of Seventh IEEE International Working Conference on Source Code Analysis and Manipulation (SCAM), pp. 163–170 (2007)
4. Porkoláb, Z., Sillye, Á.: Towards a multiparadigm complexity measure. In: 9th ECOOP Workshop on Quantitative Approaches in Object-Oriented Software Engineering (QAOOSE 2005), pp. 134–142 (2005)
5. Baudry, B., Traon, Y.L., Sunyié, G.: Testability analysis of a uml class diagram. In: 8th IEEE International Software Metrics Symposium (METRICS 2002), Ottawa, Canada, June 2002, p. 54 (2002)
6. Chidamber, R., Kemerer, C.F.: Towards a metrics suite for object oriented design. In: OOPSLA, pp. 197–211 (1991)

7. Bertoa, M.F., Troya, J.M., Vallecillo, A.: Measuring the usability of software components. Journal of Systems and Software 79(3), 427–439 (2006)
8. Moraga, M., Calero, C., Piattini, M.: Comparing different quality models for portals. Online Information Review 30(5), 555–568 (2006)
9. Neil, M., Krause, P., Fenton, N.E.: Software Quality Prediction Using Bayesian Networks. In: Software Engineering with Computational Intelligence, ch. 6. Kluwer, Dordrecht (2003)
10. Boehm, B.W., Brown, J.R., Kaspar, H., Lipow, M., Macleod, G.J., Merrit, M.J.: Characteristics of Software Quality. North-Holland, Amsterdam (1978)
11. Lange, C.F.J., Chaudron, M.R.V.: Supporting task-oriented modeling using interactive UML views. Journal of Visual Languages and Computing 18(4) (2007)
12. Atkinson, C., Bayer, J., Bunse, C., Kamsties, E., Laitenberger, O., Laqua, R., Muthig, D., Paech, B., Wüst, J., Zettel, J.: Component-based Product Line Engineering with UML. Addison Wesley, Reading (2002)

# Academic Software Development Tools and Techniques

## Report on the 1st Workshop WASDeTT at ECOOP 2008

Roel Wuyts[1], Holger M. Kienle[2], Kim Mens[3], Mark van den Brand[4],
and Adrian Kuhn[5]

[1] IMEC and KULeuven, Belgium
[2] Department of Computer Science, University of Victoria, Canada
[3] Département d'Ingénierie Informatique, Université catholique de Louvain, Belgium
[4] Mathematics and Computer Science, Eindhoven University of Technology, Netherlands
[5] Software Composition Group, University of Berne, Switzerland

**Abstract.** The objective of the 1st International Workshop on Advanced Software Development Tools and Techniques (WASDeTT-1) was to provide interested researchers with a forum to share their tool building experiences and to explore how tools can be built more effectively and efficiently. The theme for this workshop did focus on tools that target object-oriented languages and that are implemented with object-oriented languages.

This workshop report provides a brief overview of the presented tools and of the discussions that took place. The presented tools, 15 in total, covered a broad range of functionalities, among them: refactoring, modeling, behavioral specification, static and dynamic program checking, user interface composition, and program understanding. The discussion during the workshop centered around the following topics: language independent tools, tool building in an industrial context, tool building methodology, tool implementation language, and building tools with external code.

## 1   Introduction

In this paper we report on the 1st *Workshop on Academic*[1] *Software Development Tools and Techniques* (WASDeTT-1) that was held at ECOOP 2008. WASDeTT is planned as a workshop series that collocates with different conferences in the future; it is motivated by the observation that tools and tool building play an important role in applied computer science research. The tangible results of research projects are often embodied in a tool. Even though tool building is a popular technique to validate research (e.g., proof-of-concept prototyping followed by user studies), it is neither simple nor cheap to accomplish. Given the importance of tool building and the significant cost associated with it, we have initiated this workshop that allows interested researchers to share their tool building experiences and to explore how tools can be build more effectively and efficiently.

---

[1] In fact, the official title of the workshop was '*Advanced* Development Tools and Techniques' but during the workshop discussions it became clear that a more dedicated focus on 'academic' tools would have been a better choice.

P. Eugster (Ed.): ECOOP 2008 Workshop Reader, LNCS 5475, pp. 87–103, 2009.

The workshop series aims to address general topics such as the following questions:

- Should tool building remain a craft?
- Should research prototypes be of commercial quality?
- How to integrate and combine independently developed tools?
- What are the positive lessons learned in building tools?
- What are the (recurring) pitfalls in tool building?
- What are the good practices and techniques?
- Are there architectures and patterns for tool building?
- How to compare or benchmark tools?

Thus, the workshop series devotes particular attention to academic software development tools and tool building issues, where the term "development" is to be interpreted in the largest sense possible to encompass not only software development per se, but any subsequent evolution or maintenance activity.

The purpose of this workshop was *not* to focus on any specific kind of tool (say, refactoring or program comprehension tools), but rather to gather researchers working on a broad range of tools, with the goal of:

- providing a forum where tool builders—particularly, builders of experimental research prototypes—can talk about common issues relevant to the community of tool builders.
- providing a forum (workshop and associated journal) where researchers can present and explain *their* tool and thus not only get feedback on it but also real scientific credit.

Since this first edition was held at an object-oriented programming conference, all participants were working on academic tools that support *object-oriented* software development or tools that *analyze, manipulate or reason about object-oriented source code*.

Since the workshop has an interest in both tool-building issues and experimental tools themselves, two different kinds of contributions were solicited from potential participants:

1. either a traditional position paper with the participant's vision on tool-related issues;
2. or an actual tool submission where the participant will get the possibility of presenting his or her tool and how it was built.

We deliberately did not put any restrictions on the kinds of tools that are eligible for this workshop: the tools can be early prototypes, may have been around for years, or may have recently undergone a drastic re-implementation. Nevertheless, we do have a particular interest in experimental research tools (as opposed to commercial tools) and tools that target the object-oriented software development paradigm.

In spite of our focus on experimental research tools, we explicitly solicited position papers from software industrials as well. Not only will their participation in the workshop allow them to get a sneak preview of state-of-the-art research tools, their opinions and visions would allow builders of research prototypes to learn more about the actual needs of industry.

## 1.1   Origin of the Workshop and Related Workshops

The WASDeTT series builds on the experience and success of the earlier Workshop on Object-Oriented Reengineering (WOOR) series of which seven editions were co-located with ECOOP conferences. The 10th and last anniversary edition of WOOR was organized at ECOOP 2007 [1]. In spite of its specific focus on reengineering issues, WOOR traditionally gave a lot of attention to tools and tool building issues. In the last WOOR a position paper on *Must Tool Building Remain a Craft?* [2] was presented as a spring board for subsequent discussions on tool building issues in a breakout group. A result of this discussion group was that tool building issues should be further pursued within the context of a dedicated workshop series that is co-organized by the former WOOR organizers and participants, resulting in WASDeTT.

In the past, there have been other workshop that have touched on tool building issues. For example, the reverse engineering community has actively discussed tool integration in the Workshop on Standard Exchange Format[2] (WoSEF) [3] at ICSE 2000, the Dagstuhl Seminar 01041 on Interoperability of Reengineering Tools[3] in 2001, and the Workshop on Design Issues for Software Analysis and Maintenance Tools at ICSM 2005 [4]. Tool builders are increasingly leveraging external code in the form of off-the-shelf components (cf. Section 3.5). Integration issues for components is the focus of the International Workshop on Incorporating COTS-Software into Software Systems (IWICSS) that was held in 2004 at ICCBSS[4] and in 2007 at ICSE.[5]

Next to these series of workshops the journal Science of Computer Programming has devoted several special issues to academic tools and tool building. Sofar, two special issues of Experimental Software and Toolkits (EST) have been published, one in 2007 [5] and one in 2008 [6].

The observation that it is difficult to get software engineering tools adopted by industry has led to the Adoption-Centric Software Engineering (ACSE) workshop series from 2001 to 2004 [7] and more recently to the Workshop on Technology Transfer in Software Engineering [6] at ICSE 2006.

## 2   Accepted Papers

All submitted and accepted papers present academic research tools. These papers are available on the workshop web site at

```
http://smallwiki.unibe.ch/wasdett2008/submissions/
```

The tools, 15 in total, cover a broad range of topics, among them: refactoring, modeling, behavioral specification, static and dynamic program checking, user interface composition, and program comprehension. In the following, we give a brief summary

---

[2] http://www.ics.uci.edu/~ses/wosef/workshop.html
[3] http://www.dagstuhl.de/01041
[4] http://www.tuisr.utulsa.edu/iwicss/
[5] http://www.softwareml.com/IWICSS07/
[6] http://web.cecs.pdx.edu/~warren/wottse/

of the tools. In the subsequent discussion (cf. Section 3) we will refer to the tools to support our observations.

*Churrasco: Supporting Collaborative Software Evolution Analysis* [8].[7] This tool aims to support program comprehension of (distributed) development teams. It offers several visualizations that allow team members to explore software structures via an interactive web interface. Churrasco visualizes information obtained from FAMIX models, Subversion and Bugzilla.

*The MARPLE Project: A Tool for Design Pattern Detection and Software Architecture Reconstruction* [9].[8] This tool supports two reverse engineering tasks that help program comprehension, namely identification of design patterns as well as architecture reconstruction. MARPLE is realized as an Eclipse plug-in and supports systems written in Java.

*Hopscotch: Towards User Interface Composition* [10].[9] Hopscotch is an application framework and IDE of the Newspeak language. Newspeak is a dynamic language that is influenced by Smalltalk, Self and Beta, and implemented within Squeak. Hopscotch leverages Newspeak to realize a novel approach to interface composition.

*Enforcing Structural Regularities in Software using IntensiVE* [11].[10] IntensiVE is a tool suite for documenting structural source-code regularities (such as design patterns, coding conventions, etc.) in object-oriented software systems and verifying their consistency in later versions of those systems. Structural regularities are described in a declarative manner with a logic-based language.

*The mCRL2 toolset* [12].[11] mCRL2 is a behavioral specification language and toolset for describing communication behavior of software systems and to reason about them. The toolset has been used on a number of industrial case studies.

*The Rigi Reverse Engineering Environment* [13].[12] This tool supports program comprehension of software structures via a collection of fact extractors, a repository in the form of a domain-customizable exchange format, and an interactive graph visualizer. Rigi is a mature tool that is still used in research and popular in teaching, but it is currently no longer actively evolved and is in bug-fix mode.

*TestQ: Exploring Structural and Maintenance* [14].[13] The TestQ tool allows software developers to explore the structure and properties of the xUnit tests of their system with the goal to detect test smells. Test are visualized with hierarchical polymetric views that show metrics, so called smell flowers, and pie charts.

---

[7] http://churrasco.inf.unisi.ch/
[8] http://essere.disco.unimib.it/reverse/Marple.html
[9] http://newspeaklanguage.org/
[10] http://www.intensive.be
[11] http://mcrl2.org
[12] http://www.rigi.csc.uvic.ca/
[13] http://code.google.com/p/tsmells/

*The Small Project Observatory* [15].[14] The Small Project Observatory (SPO) is a visualization-based tool that supports the interactive exploration of super-repositories (i.e., repositories that host a collection of project that are developed in the context of an organization). The visualization expose relationships between projects such as developer collaborations and time-line information such a size and activity evolutions.

*Developing a Modeling Tool Using Eclipse* [16].[15] The Primus modeling tool supports the notion of architectural primitives (e.g., callback, layering, and push-pull) in software systems design. It is an Eclipse-based tool that offers modeling in UML with component diagrams enhanced with dedicated stereotypes and OCL constraints.

*Compose\*: A Language and Platform Independent Aspect Compiler for Composition Filters* [17].[16] The Compose\* framework is a compilation and execution platform for composition filters, which is a new language concept that can be applied to any programming language that supports the notion of message passing. Compose\* currently supports Java and .NET as well as C.

*The Nix Build Farm: A Declarative Approach to Continuous Integration* [18]. This tool supports the idea of continuous integration or daily builds and is used for several large projects, among them the Stratego/XT program transformation toolset. Nix features a lazy functional language to describe the building and composition of packages.

*Building a Refactoring Tool for Erlang* [19].[17] This paper describes two major versions of a refactoring tool, called RefactorErl, for the Erlang language. The authors explain features of Erlang that make fully automatic refactoring difficult or impossible (such as dynamically constructed code), describe the supported refactorings, and distill a number of tool building guidelines based on their experiences.

*Runtime Checking Java Code Using ConGu* [20].[18] ConGu is an Eclipse-based tool that allows developers to write algebraic specifications that can be then be checked during the execution of the program. ConGu's compiler takes Java class files and translates the specifications to Java Modeling Language assertions.

*CodeCity* [21].[19] CodeCity is a tool that visualizes software interactively in 3D, following a city metaphor. The buildings within the city represent classes, which are placed within districts that represent the packages. CodeCity uses building sizes, colors and transparency to enhance comprehension.

*CScout: A Refactoring Browser for C* [22].[20] CScout is a refactoring tool for C that has also support for source code analysis. It allows renaming of identifiers, but also provides hyperlinked code browsing, and form-based querying and metrics calculations

---

[14] http://evo.inf.unisi.ch:8009/spo/go/

[15] http://www.rug.nl/informatica/onderzoek/programmas/
softwareEngineering/PatternHB/tool/index

[16] http://www.ohloh.net/projects/composestar

[17] http://plc.inf.elte.hu/erlang/

[18] http://gloss.di.fc.ul.pt/congu/

[19] http://www.inf.unisi.ch/phd/wettel/codecity.html

[20] http://www.spinellis.gr/cscout/

on identifiers, functions, and files. CScout has been used on large software systems such as the Linux kernel.

The presented tools cover the whole software life cycle, ranging from system modeling (Primus) and behavioral specification (mCRL2), to frameworks for novel programming paradigms (Compose*) and user interface design (Hopscotch), to build support for a software system (Nix), to checking of programs based on static analysis (IntensiVE) and run-time execution (ConGu), to refactoring of programs (RefactorErl and CScout), and to program comprehension (Churrasco, MARPLE, Rigi, TestQ, SPO, and CodeCity).

Tools for program comprehension were especially well represented at the workshop. All of these tools offer visualizations that help to understand the structure and properties of a software system. Traditionally, program comprehension tools have extracted static dependencies of a single snapshot of a target system. This is the case for both Rigi and MARPLE. Program comprehension tools have extended functionalities in various directions. For example, they mine source code for particular code patterns or bad smells (MARPLE and TestQ), they extract information from more diverse sources such as bug-tracking systems (Churrasco), they look at multiple snapshots and track the evolution of a system over time (SPO and CodeCity), and they broaden their scope from a single system to super-repositories (SPO).

## 3    Workshop Structure and Outcomes

The workshop featured presentations of all 15 tools. In order to allow sufficient time for discussion, three tools were selected for longer presentations of 20 minutes each (i.e., IntensiVE, Churrasco, and Hopscotch) while the other tools were discussed in 7 minute lighting talks (a.k.a. "blitz" presentations). The longer presentations allowed room for a formal tool demo and were chosen because they seemed promising to give rise to interesting interactions and discussions.

Presenters were instructed that they should introduce their tool in a nutshell (i.e., its purpose, its strength and its main weaknesses) and to then focus on tool builder issues (i.e., lessons learned that are of interest for fellow tool builders). Each talk was followed by a short round of discussion that allowed for a few questions.

After the talks a short plenary discussion took place in order to plan the interactive part of the workshop. The following topics were proposed by organizers and participants:

(i) **language independent tools:** How can we build tools that work across multiple languages?

(ii) **tool building in an industrial context:** How to build tools that get accepted in industry?

(iii) **data interoperability among tools:** How to exchange data between tools and how to process this data?

(iv) **maturation of tools:** How to grow a tool from an early prototype into a mature tool or framework?

(v) **tool building methodology:** How—and to what degree—can we adopt established software engineering techniques for building research tools?

**(vi) tool building in teams:** How to build tools in larger—and possibly distributed—teams?

**(vii) tool implementation language:** How does the choice of a programming language impact the building of a tool, its usability, and the context in which the tool can be applied?

It was decided to pick the four most popular topics from the above list by vote, and to allocate about 25 minutes for discussion for each topic. Each of the organizers did introduce and moderate one topic. The selected topics were (i), (ii), (v) and (vii) and the discussions are summarized in Sections 3.1–3.4, respectively.

By polling the audience we found that nearly everybody was actively engaged in tool building or had concrete tool building experiences. This high level of expertise was reflected by engaging and lively discussions.

During the decision on the topics a discussion ensued about the observation that a significant number of tools depend on external code in the form of other tools, libraries, or frameworks. This discussion is summarized and expanded upon in Section 3.5.

## 3.1 Language Independent Tools

Language independence is an important feature for a tool. It is equally important for tool users as well as tool developers. From a user perspective, a tool that can be applied to a portfolio of languages can be an important incentive because once the general principles of a tool are understood, it can be applied to a larger variety of different software systems. From a developer perspective, deciding on the target language(s) is an important research decision that also can have a significant impact on the design and architecture of the tool.

To better understand the issue of language independence, it is instructive to look at the history of reverse engineering tools. Many reverse engineering tools, especially the ones developed in the late 80s and early 90s, supported only a single programming language (e.g., MasterScope for Lisp, FAST for Fortran, and Cscope for C [23]). Since these tools consisted of a single front end, there was often a tight coupling between the targeted language and the rest of the system [24]. This rather tight coupling was often not intentional and thus not realized by the tool builders. Adding of a new front end for a different language, which should have been a conceptually simple task, proved in practice to be quite difficult or infeasible. This observation led to the proposal of a clean separation between extraction and analysis by means of a language-independent, general representation that captures the semantics of multiple source languages [24].[21]

Language independent representations enable a decoupling of the processing for different source languages from subsequent analyses. The vision here is that analyses can operate across all of the source languages without modification. But can we come up with a (intermediate) language that we can use to represent and reason about all languages? One approach to tackle this question is based on the observation that it depends

---

[21] Note the similarity to the domain of compiler construction. For instance, UNCOL was an attempt to define a unified, executable intermediate representation for diverse programming languages.

on the purpose of the language and the tools that leverage the language. Important considerations are for instance:

- semantic rigor of the language elements
- granularity of the language elements
- abstractions that generalize over elements of different languages
- characteristics and diversity of the targeted languages

The more semantic precision we demand from a language, the more difficult it becomes to define and describe such a language. Semantic rigor is needed if the tool has to support sound analyses (such as fully automated code transformations). In this case, the language needs to be fine grained (i.e., allowing to express information at the level of abstract syntax trees and control flow graphs). Examples of such tools are IntensiVE, ConGu, and CScout. In contrast, there are tools that do neither require sound analyses nor fine-grained information. This is the case for program understanding and reverse engineering tools that provide abstractions over the target language such as Rigi, TestQ, and CodeCity. For such kinds of tools language independent representations seem
feasible.

The FAMIX meta-model of the Moose tool provides a language-independent representation of object-oriented features, the core model, which can be extended with language-specific information via subclassing. FAMIX's core model consists of entities to represent classes, methods, attributes, method invocations, field accesses, and inheritance relationships. A weak approach to language independence is provided by Rigi's exchange format, called RSF. RSF enables to define a meta-model via attaching types in the form of labels to nodes and arcs. Multiple meta-models can be shared by following naming conventions on the type names. However, both FAMIX and RSF are so-called "middle-level" representations; they have not been designed for the representation of fine-grained information and as a consequence are not suitable for this purpose.

To achieve language independence it is necessary to find suitable abstractions that generalize over multiple languages. In this respect, the challenge for a suitable language independent representation is to find appropriate abstractions that preserve the needed semantic rigor over multiple languages. The IntensiVE tool for example provides abstractions in the form of intentions over properties of the source code. Another example of abstraction are intermediate representations such as Java bytecode and .NET CIL that are targeted by a number of diverse languages.

However, finding suitable abstractions can be difficult or may turn out to be infeasible. This leads to the observation that language independence should not be pursued at all cost. From a research perspective, language independence is often not a crucial requirement. For example, validation of a novel research idea with a tool prototype can focus typically on a single language. From an economic perspective, it may be more cost effective to re-implement functionality for a new source language instead of expending the effort of first redesigning the system for language independence to then benefit from the reuse of the language independent code. An approach to simplify retargeting for a new language is model-driven development. The authors of the Refactor-Erl tool follow this approach and describes it as follows: "This is a declarative approach which maintains the refactoring-specific lexical, syntactical and static semantical rules of the investigated language as data. Modifying these data should result in the (as far as possible) automatic adaptation of the code of all the components of the refactoring tool" [19].

It seems important that researchers clarify the term language independent because it has different meanings. For example, language independence could mean that the tool is designed in such manner that it is feasible to support a new language. Depending on the language, this may require more or less effort. In practice, this often means that it is only feasible to add a language that has certain characteristics; for instance, the language may have to support a certain paradigm such as object-oriented or procedural as opposed to functional, or it may have to be statically typed as opposed to dynamically typed. Furthermore, language independence could also mean that the tool works on any or most kinds of languages because it abstracts away from language-specific features. This approach is pursued by lexically-based clone detection tool such as CCFinder. Last, language independence could also mean that the tool targets systems that are composed of multiple (programming) languages. One approach to effectively support multiple languages is to integrate them into a common meta-model (e.g., GUPRO [25] and the ASF+SDF Meta-Environment [26]).

From a practical engineering point of view, it may be better to focus on implementing full support for one language first, and then to add support for multiple languages later on. However, language independence should be taken into account as an important requirement from the start when designing and architecting the tool.

## 3.2 Tool Building in an Industrial Context

Transforming academic tools into commercial tools involves quite some effort. The best way is to do this outside the academic environment, in a so-called spin-off company. There are quite a number of success stories but also quite a number of failures. The Software Improvement Group [22] is an example of a very successful spin-off company. This company made a commercial product of the DocGen tooling [27] and applied this tooling to quite a number of large-scale projects. The original idea of selling the DocGen tooling was transformed into selling consultancy based on the DocGen tooling. The advantage of this way of working is that the requirements on the DocGen tooling were less severe since the users are always (in-house) experts.

RefactorErl [19] is an example of a tool that was built for an industrial partner (in this case Ericsson) on demand. This a very fortunate situation which is established via a long lasting cooperation between this company and the university. Such an opportunity enables a quick transformation of research ideas into a commercially relevant tooling. However, the risk is that the university is transformed into a company. Furthermore, it puts some responsibility on the developers with respect to maintenance of the tooling.

The application of academic tools in an industrial context is in general not trivial. There are two main reasons for this phenomena. The most important one is the level of maturity of the academic tools. In most cases the academic tools are prototypes and application on industrial scale usually involves quite some effort. In some cases it means a complete reimplementation of the tooling. Second, the industry wants guarantees about support, maintenance, documentation, training, etc. Commercial tools and tool vendors

---

[22] http://www.sig.nl

can and will offer this support whereas in an academic setting quite often one is depending on a small-scale development team.

In a recent large-scale research project, "Ideals," [23] one of the goals was to use industry-as-laboratory. The tools and methodology developed in this research project had to be deployed at the industrial partner ASML [24], a company which builds and sells high-tech products (waffersteppers). They have a huge code base and the scope of this research project was to improve the maintainability of the code base. Besides performing research the goal of the project was to transition the developed technology as fast as possible to the company. The encountered problems were in the area of finding managers who wanted to participate in applying this new technology, furthermore the maturity of tooling, development of documentation and development of teaching material were considered as problematic. Eventually, one or two research results were transferred to ASML.

In the middle of the 90's ASF+SDF [26] was used to prototype a domain specific language for describing financial products [28]. This work was done in cooperation with a Dutch bank and a large software company. The specifications and generated C-code was transferred to both the bank and software company. This software company sold this product to another Dutch bank. Around 2005 a small problem in the software was detected and this triggered some maintenance on the specification. Fortunately, we had still the original specifications because the software company had thrown away the specifications and only kept the generated C-files. The reason for this was that they did not understand the specifications and thought they were not important.

These examples show that transferring academic tooling to industry is a huge effort that should not be underestimated. The success of the transfer depends on many factors but the most important ones are commitment of the company and commitment of the researchers involved.

### 3.3   Tool Building Methodology

The developers of research tools in computer science are quite often also involved in teaching courses on programming and software engineering. The traditional software engineering courses address topics like, requirements engineering, design, architecture, coding (standards), testing, software process, etc. Do we apply (some of) these techniques when developing our academic software? Only a few participants indicate that they have used, or should use some of the established software engineering techniques. Of course, the underlying hypothesis is that the quality of the software and the efficiency of development increases when applying software engineering techniques, which leaves more time for writing (scientific) papers.

There are examples of dedicated processes that have been proposed for industrial researching and academic tool building. Extreme Researching (XR) is a process specifically designed for applied research and development in a distributed environment that has to cope with changing human resources and rapid prototyping [29]. It is an adaptation of Extreme Programming (XP) and has been developed by Ericsson Applied

---

[23] http://www.esi.nl/Ideals

[24] http://www.asml.com

Research Laboratories to support distributed telecommunications research. XR is based on several core principles taken from XP (short development cycles, test-driven development, collective ownership, and discipline) and encodes them in a set of activities (e.g., remote pair programming, unit testing, collective knowledge, coding standards, frequent integration, and metaphor). Dedicated tool support is available for XR with a web-based portal. Notably, the authors of XR estimate, based on three projects, that their process has yielded an increase of output of around 24% and reduced project-overrun time on average by half. Kienle and Müller explore the current state of tool building practices in academia with the aim to improve upon the state-of-the-art [30]. Based on a literature survey, they propose a number of desirable characteristics for a process in academia. Such a process should be feedback-based (soliciting of input from users), iterative (as opposed to waterfall), prototype-based, lightweight (minimizing of artifacts), and adaptive (to accommodate changing project requirements). Based on the identified requirements, they introduce a tailorable process framework based on work products. The work products address issues such as tool requirements (both functional and non-functional), prototyping (technical and user interface prototype), and tool architecture. A tailorable framework is needed because "the individual [tool] projects seem too diverse to be accommodated by a single, one-size-fits-all process" [30].

It appears that modern software engineering techniques, such as agile development principles, are more frequently applied by researchers when building their tooling. A considerable number of participants indicate that they use (unit) testing and everybody uses version management systems. One of the reasons not to use traditional software engineering techniques is related to the domain: you do not know what you will need to do, so it is hard to write a requirements document up-front. So you start with a vague idea, a prototype, and you extend it. So agile development works better in a research context: you discover more of the exact problem domain as you go with your research. In a research context even a full-fledged agile development methodology (let alone a heavier process) can even be too structured specially when developing prototypes to support (scientific) papers, however as soon as a tool becomes increasingly popular and is used by other researchers, a more structured approach to software development is needed.

In this context, the following question is of interest: Do universities rather produce people that are good developers or good researchers? In order to perform good research—especially in the domain of software engineering—it may be necessary to develop good software. Furthermore, is the difference between industry and academia that big? Quite often industry applies agile software development even when the official policy is a heavy software process. The freedom in academic software development is also relative. If your tool becomes a success, the freedom in development is gone. In this case, you have pressure to provide architectural descriptions and good documentation, and you even may have to freeze interfaces or features. User want to have stable tooling and fellow developers want to have a stable architecture. But it is also important to have well-defined and stable interfaces, so that other developers and researcher can develop their own components. It is not bad to start with a small quick-and-dirty prototype for a paper, but when do you decide that it makes sense to set up Bugzilla, write architectural documentation, introduce coding standards, etc. If you start introducing more formality into your tool development too early, it may end up being a waste of time and unnecessarily bogging down the rapid prototyping of tool functionality; if you introduce it too late you may waste time and resources as well because the tool architecture, interfaces and the code have to go through a major restructuring in order to stabilize further development.

The overall conclusion is that application of rigorous software engineering principles is not (always) possible, but some agreement on principles, architecture, and tooling can safe a lot of time and energy. So, everybody needs to use the techniques that fits for them best—as long as they are made explicit.

### 3.4  Tool Implementation Language

Perhaps most importantly, never forget why you are building your prototype. If it is built for the sole purpose to validate a research idea then you can create your tool as a prototype in whatever language that allows you to be most productive so that you can focus on your research contribution and not your tool. For example, the implementation of SOUL was done in Smalltalk, which was an appropriate approach because the goal was to demonstrate how a logic language can be integrated with an object-oriented language, and how the logic language can then be used as a meta-programming language for that object-oriented language. In this context, there was no benefit in implementing SOUL in a more efficient language such as C++ or more popular language such as Java. Note also that if industry decides to pick up research ideas embodied in your prototype, regardless of the language it is implemented in, it will be rewritten anyway.

Certain language features can be quite helpful for tool design. For example, C++ generics in combination with the Standard Template Library (STL) can simplify the experimentation with different strategies or algorithms. For example, the authors of mCRL2 say that "primary motivations for the choice of C++ were advanced language facilities for creating library interfaces, the availability of the C++ Standard Library, and facilities for generic programming. Generic programming not only reduces the duplication of code, it also makes it easier to adapt algorithms" [12]. On the downside, the author of CScout reports that the use of STL complicates debugging with gdb because "gdb provides a view of the data structures' implementation details, but not their high-level operations" [22].

Another ingredient when selecting the implementation language can be the principle of "eating your own dog food." The ASF+SDF Meta-Environment [26] is an environment for developing language descriptions, both syntax as well as semantics. A number of components (e.g., parse table generator, compiler, and well-formedness checker of SDF definitions) in this system are developed using ASF+SDF itself. This approach enables the immediate checking of functionality and expressiveness of the underlying formalism.

The choice of the implementation language is of course also influenced by education. If the students are mostly or exclusively introduced to Java in their courses, it is likely that when they become researchers they will develop their software in Java as well. This can be a drawback. The first version of the ASF+SDF Meta-Environment was implemented in Lisp, a very popular language in the 80's for prototyping. Researchers that joint the project later on were not so familiar with Lisp and this caused quite some problems when doing maintenance.

**Table 1.** The presented tools and the components that they are leveraging

| Tool | Leveraged Components |
|------|----------------------|
| Churrasco | FAMIX (meta-model), MOOSE (fact extraction), GLORP (repository), SVG (visualization) |
| MARPLE | Eclipse: JDT (Java fact extraction), GEF (visualization), Glassfish (distributed computing), Weka (clustering) |
| Hopscotch | Smalltalk |
| IntensiVE | Eclipse JDT (Java fact extraction), javaconnect (interoperability from Smalltalk to Java), SOUL (querying), Mondrian (visualization), Star Browser (user interface) |
| mCRL2 | ATerms (repository), Boost (utility), C++ Standard Library (utility) |
| Rigi | Yacc (C fact extractor), Tk (user interface), GraphEd (graph layout) |
| TestQ | Fetch toolchain: Source Navigator (fact extraction), CDIF2RSF (format transformation), pmccabe (C/C++ metrics), JavaNSCC (Java metrics), Crocopat (querying), Guess (visualization) |
| SPO | MOOSE (fact extraction), Seaside (user interface), SVG (visualization) |
| Primus | Eclipse: OCL (modeling support), UML2 (user interface), UML2Tools (visualization) |
| Nix Build Farm | ATerms (term rewriting) |
| RefactorErl | XML (configuration), Emacs (user interface) |
| ConGu | Eclipse (user interface) |
| CodeCity | FAMIX (meta-model), MOOSE (Smalltalk fact extraction), iPlasma (Java/C++ fact extraction), MSE exchange format (repository), Jun/OpenGL (visualization) |
| CScout | BtYacc (C fact extractor), STL (utility), mySQL (repository and querying), dot (visualization) |

## 3.5 Building Tools with External Code

It seems that researchers are increasingly leveraging components to assemble their tools instead of building them from scratch. In fact, this is reflected by most of the presented tools. Table 1 shows the workshop's tools along with examples of the components that they are leveraging in order to realize the tools' functionalities. We use the term *components* to denote external code that is packaged in such a way that reuse is facilitated. In this context, a suitable working definition of a component is given by Meyer, who characterizes it as "an element of software that can be used by many different applications" [31, page 1200]. Leveraging components for tool building has been dubbed component-based tool development (CBTD) [32].

There are many examples of suitable components that can be used for tool building. Drawing from the components in Table 1, we can classify components according to standard functionalities as follows:

**repository:** Tools typically need to store information in some form or another. This can be accomplished with exchange formats such as Moose's MSE[33] (CodeCity), ATerms [34] (mCRL2), the Rigi Standard Format (RSF), CDIF (TestQ), or XML (MARPLE); alternatively, tools can leverage relational databases (CScout uses mySQL and PostgreSQL) or object-relational database mappers (Churrasco uses

GLORP[25]). An advantage of using repository components is that they often have some form of modeling support and also come with a query and/or transformation language. For example, support for modeling of information about source code is provided by FAMIX[26] and Rigi.

**fact extraction:** Tools for software engineering have to extract information about the target system. Almost all presented tools extract static information from source code (as opposed to dynamic information collected during program execution). Since the building of extractors for complex languages such as C++ is a time-consuming and error-prone task, many tools rely on external fact extractors. For example, TestQ relies on SourceNavigator. CodeCity uses MOOSE for Smalltalk and iPlasma[27] for C++ and Java code. MARPLE and IntensiVE query the parse tree of the Eclipse JDT. One can also use parser generators to simply the construction of a custom extractor. Rigi has a parser for C that is based on Yacc (no longer supported), and CScout's parser is based on BtYacc.[28]

**user interface and visualization:** Tools have to provide some form of visualization and user interface to show and manipulate information. Several tools offer user interfaces based on web technology. CScout has a simple HTML-based interface while Churrasco and SPO have more sophisticated Web 2.0 like interfaces. Both Churrasco and SPO use Scalable Vector Graphics (SVG) with JavaScript for interactive visualizations. SPO also uses the Seaside[29] web application framework. Another popular strategy is to integrated the tool with an IDE. Several tools are realized as Eclipse plug-ins (MARPLE, Primus, and ConGu), while RefactorErl leverages Emacs. To visualize software structures several tools use interactive graph editors. IntensiVE is based on the Mondrian[30] visualization engine, TestQ is based on GUESS,[31] and MARPLE uses the Eclipse Graphical Editing Framework (GEF). In contrast, CScout provides static graphs based on dot.

**data structures and algorithms:** General utility libraries for data structures and algorithms can reduce implementation effort for tools. Both mCRL2 and CScout are implemented in C++ and use its Standard Library extensively.

An interesting question that should be further pursued is to what extent CBTD differs from implementing tools from scratch, and what are the potential benefits and drawbacks of both development approaches? The developers of the Primus tool report several lessons learned of building their tool on top of Eclipse [16]. For example, plugin-in develop can be challenging because of lack of in-depth documentation and code examples. Available plug-ins can vary considerably in their maturity and immature plug-ins may evolve rapidly and have unstable APIs. Also, APIs of plug-ins may not be powerful or flexible enough. For example, the OCL editor plug-in does not provide sufficient

---

[25] http://www.glorp.org
[26] http://www.iam.unibe.ch/~famoos/FAMIX/
[27] http://loose.upt.ro/iplasma/
[28] http://www.siber.com/btyacc/
[29] http://www.seaside.st/
[30] http://moose.unibe.ch/tools/mondrian
[31] http://graphexploration.cond.org/

detail about query errors for Primus' purposes. On the positive side, the Eclipse online community is active and responsive.

## 4 Conclusion and Outlook

The first WASDeTT turned out to be a stimulating event with 15 presentations that covered a variety of software engineering tools, formal tool demos as part of several presentations, and thought-provoking discussions among the participants. The discussed topics—language independent tools, tool building in an industrial context, tool building methodology, tool implementation language, and tool building with external code— showed that tool building issues are of interest to many researchers. This workshop generated first promising results, but it seems worthwhile to further pursue these discussion topics in subsequent workshops. Indeed, the 2nd WASDeTT[32] was already held (collocated with ICSM 2008), which had a special focus on tool building in an industrial context with four invited talks.

We already made the point that one important goal of this workshop series is to enable researchers to publish about their tools so that they can get scientific credit for their tool building efforts. To further this goal, a selection of the best tool submissions will be published in a special issue on *Experimental Software Toolkits* (EST) of Elsevier's *Science of Computer Programming* journal [5]. Two organizers of this workshop (Mark van den Brand and Kim Mens) will act as the editors of this EST issue.

## Acknowledgments

Many thanks to the workshop presenters and participants. We also gratefully acknowledge the dedicated work of the program committee.

## References

1. Demeyer, S., Guéhéneuc, Y.G., Mens, K., Wuyts, R., Ducasse, S., Gall, H. (eds.): Proceedings of the ECOOP 2007 Workshop on Object-Oriented Re-engineering (WOOR 2007) – 10th anniversary edition (2007), http://smallwiki.unibe.ch/woor2007/
2. Kienle, H.M.: Must tool building remain a craft? In: Demeyer, S., Guéhéneuc, Y.G., Mens, K., Wuyts, R., Ducasse, S., Gall, H. (eds.) Proceedings of the ECOOP 2007 Workshop on Object-Oriented Re-engineering (WOOR 2007) – 10th anniversary edition (2007)
3. Sim, S.E., Koschke, R.: WoSEF: Workshop on standard exchange format. IEEE Software Engineering Notes 26(1), 44–49 (2001)
4. Jin, D.: Design issues for software analysis and maintenance tools. In: IEEE International Workshop on Software Technology and Engineering Practice (STEP 2005), pp. 115–117 (2005)
5. van den Brand, M.: Guest editor's introduction: Experimental software and toolkits (EST). Science of Computer Programming 69(1–3), 1–2 (2007)
6. van den Brand, M.: Guest editor's introduction: Second issue of experimental software and toolkits (EST). Science of Computer Programming 71(1–2), 1–2 (2008)

---

[32] http://wasdett2.wikispaces.com/

7. Balzer, B., Litoiu, M., Müller, H., Smith, D., Storey, M., Tilley, S., Wong, K.: 4th International Workshop on Adoption-Centric Software Engineering (ACSE 2004), pp. 1–2 (2004)
8. D'Ambros, M., Lanza, M.: Churrasco: Supporting collaborative software evolution analysis. In: Mens, K., van den Brand, M., Kuhn, A., Kienle, H.M., Wuyts, R. (eds.) 1st International Workshop on Academic Software Development Tools and Techniques (WASDeTT-1) (2008)
9. Arcelli, F., Tosi, C., Zanoni, M., Maggioni, S.: The MARPLE project: A tool for design pattern detection and software architecture reconstruction. In: Mens, K., van den Brand, M., Kuhn, A., Kienle, H.M., Wuyts, R. (eds.) 1st International Workshop on Academic Software Development Tools and Techniques (WASDeTT-1) (2008)
10. Boykov, V.: Hopscotch: Towards user interface composition. In: Mens, K., van den Brand, M., Kuhn, A., Kienle, H.M., Wuyts, R. (eds.) 1st International Workshop on Academic Software Development Tools and Techniques (WASDeTT-1) (2008)
11. Brichau, J., Kellens, A., Castro, S., D'Hondt, T.: Enforcing structural regularities in software using IntensiVE. In: Mens, K., van den Brand, M., Kuhn, A., Kienle, H.M., Wuyts, R. (eds.) 1st International Workshop on Academic Software Development Tools and Techniques (WASDeTT-1) (2008)
12. Groote, J.F., Keiren, J., Mathijssen, A., Ploeger, B., Stappers, F., Tankink, C., Usenko, Y., van Weerdenburg, M., Wesselink, W., Willemse, T., van der Wulp, J.: The mCRL2 toolset. In: Mens, K., van den Brand, M., Kuhn, A., Kienle, H.M., Wuyts, R. (eds.) 1st International Workshop on Academic Software Development Tools and Techniques (WASDeTT-1) (2008)
13. Kienle, H.M., Müller, H.A.: The Rigi reverse engineering environment. In: Mens, K., van den Brand, M., Kuhn, A., Kienle, H.M., Wuyts, R. (eds.) 1st International Workshop on Academic Software Development Tools and Techniques (WASDeTT-1) (2008)
14. Breugelmans, M., Rompaey, B.V.: TestQ: Exploring structural and maintenance characteristics of unit test suites. In: Mens, K., van den Brand, M., Kuhn, A., Kienle, H.M., Wuyts, R. (eds.) 1st International Workshop on Academic Software Development Tools and Techniques (WASDeTT-1) (2008)
15. Lungu, M., Lanza, M.: The small project observatory. In: Mens, K., van den Brand, M., Kuhn, A., Kienle, H.M., Wuyts, R. (eds.) 1st International Workshop on Academic Software Development Tools and Techniques (WASDeTT-1) (2008)
16. Kamal, A.W., Kirtley, N., Avgeriou, P.: Developing a modeling tool using Eclipse. In: Mens, K., van den Brand, M., Kuhn, A., Kienle, H.M., Wuyts, R. (eds.) 1st International Workshop on Academic Software Development Tools and Techniques (WASDeTT-1) (2008)
17. de Roo, A., Hendriks, M., Havinga, W., Durr, P., Bergmans, L.: Compose*: A language and platform independent aspect compiler for composition filters. In: Mens, K., van den Brand, M., Kuhn, A., Kienle, H.M., Wuyts, R. (eds.) 1st International Workshop on Academic Software Development Tools and Techniques (WASDeTT-1) (2008)
18. Dolstra, E., Visser, E.: The Nix Build Farm: A declarative approach to continuous integration. In: Mens, K., van den Brand, M., Kuhn, A., Kienle, H.M., Wuyts, R. (eds.) 1st International Workshop on Academic Software Development Tools and Techniques (WASDeTT-1) (2008)
19. Horváth, Z., Lovei, L., Kozsik, T., Kitlei, R.: Building a refactoring tool for Erlang. In: Mens, K., van den Brand, M., Kuhn, A., Kienle, H.M., Wuyts, R. (eds.) 1st International Workshop on Academic Software Development Tools and Techniques (WASDeTT-1) (2008)
20. Vasconcelos, V.T., Nunes, I., Lopes, A., Ramiro, N., Crispim, P.: Runtime checking Java code using ConGu. In: Mens, K., van den Brand, M., Kuhn, A., Kienle, H.M., Wuyts, R. (eds.) 1st International Workshop on Academic Software Development Tools and Techniques (WASDeTT-1) (2008)
21. Wettel, R., Lanza, M.: CodeCity. In: Mens, K., van den Brand, M., Kuhn, A., Kienle, H.M., Wuyts, R. (eds.) 1st International Workshop on Academic Software Development Tools and Techniques (WASDeTT-1) (2008)

22. Spinellis, D.: CScout: A refactoring browser for C. In: Mens, K., van den Brand, M., Kuhn, A., Kienle, H.M., Wuyts, R. (eds.) 1st International Workshop on Academic Software Development Tools and Techniques (WASDeTT-1) (2008)

23. Chen, Y., Nishimoto, M.Y., Ramamoorthy, C.V.: The C information abstraction system. IEEE Transactions on Software Engineering 16(3), 325–334 (1990)

24. Reubenstein, H., Piazza, R., Roberts, S.: Separating parsing and analysis in reverse engineering. In: 1st IEEE Working Conference on Reverse Engineering (WCRE 1993), pp. 117–125 (1993)

25. Kullbach, B., Winter, A., Dahm, P., Ebert, J.: Program comprehension in multi-language systems. In: 5th IEEE Working Conference on Reverse Engineering (WCRE 1998), pp. 135–143 (1998)

26. van den Brand, M., Bruntink, M., Economopoulos, G., de Jong, H., Klint, P., Kooiker, T., van der Storm, T., Vinju, J.: Using The Meta-environment for Maintenance and Renovation. In: Proceedings of the 11th European Conference on Software Maintenance and Reengineering (CSMR 2007), pp. 331–332. IEEE Computer Society Press, Los Alamitos (2007)

27. Deursen, A., Kuipers, T.: Building documentation generators. In: Proceedings International Conference on Software Maintenance, pp. 40–49. IEEE Computer Society, Los Alamitos (1999)

28. van den Brand, M., van Deursen, A., Klint, P., Klusener, S., van den Meulen, E.: Industrial applications of ASF+SDF. In: Wirsing, M., Nivat, M. (eds.) AMAST 1996. LNCS, vol. 1101. Springer, Heidelberg (1996)

29. Chirouze, O., Cleary, D., Mitchell, G.G.: A software methodology for applied research: eXtreme Researching. Software—Practice and Experience 35(15), 1441–1454 (2005)

30. Kienle, H.M., Müller, H.A.: Towards a process for developing maintenance tools in academia. In: 15th IEEE Working Conference on Reverse Engineering (WCRE 2008), pp. 237–246 (2008)

31. Meyer, B.: Object-Oriented Software Construction, 2nd edn. Prentice-Hall, Englewood Cliffs (1997)

32. Kienle, H.M.: Component-based tool development. In: Frontiers of Software Maintenance (FoSM) at ICSM 2008 (2008)

33. Kuhn, A., Verwaest, T.: FAME, a polyglot library for metamodeling at runtime. In: Workshop on Models at Runtime, n. 10 (2008)

34. van den Brand, M., de Jong, H., Klint, P., Olivier, P.: Efficient Annotated Terms. Software, Practice & Experience 30, 259–291 (2000)

# Parallel/High-Performance Object-Oriented Scientific Computing: Today's Research, Tomorrow's Practice
## Report on the 7th POOSC Workshop, ECOOP 2008

Kei Davis[1] and Jörg Striegnitz[2]

[1] Los Alamos National Laboratory, Los Alamos, NM 87545, USA
kei.davis@lanl.gov
http://www.ccs3.lanl.gov/~kei/
[2] University Of Applied Sciences Regensburg 93053 Regensburg, Germany
joerg.striegnitz@informtik.fh-regensburg.de
http://homepages.fh-regensburg.de/~stj39817/

**Abstract.** While object-oriented programming has been embraced in industry, particularly in the form of C++, Java, and Python, its acceptance by the parallel scientific programming community is for various reasons incomplete. Nonetheless, various factors practically dictate the use of language features that provide higher level abstractions than do C or older FORTRAN standards. These include increasingly complex physics models, numerical algorithms, and hardware (e.g. deep memory hierarchies, ever-increasing numbers of processors, and the advent of multi- and many-core processors and heterogeneous architectures). Our emphases are on identifying specific problems impeding greater acceptance and widespread use of object-oriented programming in scientific computing; proposed and implemented solutions to these problems; and new or novel frameworks, approaches, techniques, or idioms for parallel/high-performance object-oriented scientific computing.

**Keywords:** Parallel computing, high-performance computing, scientific computing, object-oriented computing.

## 1 Introduction

We start by motivating the appropriateness of an ongoing workshop series on parallel/high-performance object-oriented scientific computing, giving a brief history of the workshop series, and stating our current working purview via the current abstract.

### 1.1 Motivation

Ever-increasing compute capability has enabled scientific programming to reach an unprecedented degree of sophistication and complexity. Complex algorithms,

P. Eugster (Ed.): ECOOP 2008 Workshop Reader, LNCS 5475, pp. 104–115, 2009.

a wide range of hardware environments, and an increasing demand for software system modularity, portability, and fault tolerance have shown that language-level abstraction must increase. At the same time, because the achievable capability of the highest-end machines defines the achievable limits of size and fidelity of scientific simulations, performance cannot be compromised.

Concurrently with entering the petaflop era we are experiencing an unprecented growth in the use of computational accelerators and heterogeneous architectures, currently including field-programmable gate arrays (FPGAs), graphics processing units (GPUs), ClearSpeed floating point accelerators, and IBM's Cell Broadband Engine, among others. Most programming for these devices is 'at the metal,' and much research is being conducted to provide productive and performant abstractions of the low-level models these architectures present.

Work presented at previous POOSC workshops has shown that the OO approach provides an effective means for the design of highly complex scientific systems, and that it is possible to design abstractions and applications that fulfill strict performance requirements. However, OO isn't fully embraced in high performance computing, and there is still demand for, and interest in, active research in this field. Previous POOSC workshops have proven that a workshop is an ideal venue for communicating active research activities, that new approaches and techniques are constantly being developed, and that researchers and developers are keen to share these in a live, interactive setting.

## 1.2  History

The current organizers, with various changes in personnel over the years, have organized successful POOSC workshops several times, once at OOPSLA'01 and the others at previous ECOOP conferences. Response to the CFP has always been sufficiently good that a formal reviewing and selection process needed to be imposed. The workshops themselves have been lively forums for debate and discussion and have resulted in a number of new collaborations.

## 2  Summary of Call for Participation

While object-oriented programming is being embraced in industry, particularly in the form of C++ and to an increasing extent Java and Python, its acceptance by the parallel scientific programming community is still tentative. In this latter domain performance is invariably of paramount importance, where even C++ is considered suspect, primarily because of real or perceived loss of performance. On the other hand, various factors practically dictate the use of language features that provide higher level abstractions than do C or older FORTRAN standards. These include increasingly complex physics models, numerical algorithms, and hardware–deep memory hierarchies, exponentially-increasing numbers of processors, and the advent of multi- and many-core processors and heterogeneous architectures.

This workshop seeks to bring together practitioners and researchers in this growing field to present and discuss their work. The emphasis is on identifying specific problems impeding greater acceptance and widespread use of object-oriented programming in scientific computing; proposed and implemented solutions to these problems; and new or novel approaches, techniques or idioms for scientific and/or parallel computing. Presentations of work in progress are welcome.

Specific areas of interest include, but are not limited to:

- tried or proposed programming language alternatives to C++;
- performance issues and their realized or proposed resolution;
- issues specific to handling or abstracting parallelism, including the handling or abstraction of heterogeneous architectures;
- specific points of concern for progress and acceptance of object-oriented scientific computing;
- existing, developing, or proposed software;
- frameworks and tools for scientific object-oriented computing;
- schemes for user-level fault tolerance;
- grand visions (of relevance).

The workshop will consist of a sequences of presentations each followed by a discussion session. The workshop will conclude with an overall discussion. We expect the majority of the participants to give presentations.

## 3    Participants and Presentation Topics

This section briefly describes each of the presentations, and attempts to put each in a larger context motivating the problems to be solved.

**Réza Ansari.** presented the SOPHYA class library, a collection of C++ classes designed for intensive numerical and physics data analysis. SOPHYA provides a comprehensive set of data containers, such as multi-dimensional arrays, vectors, matrices, histograms, and tables, covering common areas of scientific simulation and data analysis. Transparent and efficient memory management are among the salient features of the library. Indeed, in order to avoid expensive data copies, SOPHYA classes managing large objects implement automatic reference sharing and memory management. Significantly, the SOPHYA memory management and reference sharing services are thread-safe.

Persistence and efficient data import/export are among the important services provided by SOPHYA. SOPHYA provides data import/export, through delegate classes, in a format (FITS) widely used in the astronomical community. SOPHYA was shown to perform efficiently compared to low level coding or similar libraries.

Also showcased was the *spiapp* multi-threaded interactive data analysis tool, built on top of SOPHYA library, a C++ graphics and GUI object library (PI) and an extendable object framework (PIext) encapsulating the library data objects. *Spiapp* is able to execute C++ code fragments via PIext services, in particular in-the-fly code compilation and linking.

**Markus Blatt.** Large-scale parallel codes typically require data to be decomposed among the set of processes active in the computation. A given data decomposition usually implies a recurring communication scheme. Typical examples are parallel data decomposition methods and finite element computations on unstructured grids.

Markus Blatt presented *Generic C++ Components for Data-Parallel Computations*, which introduces generic template classes in C++ for describing (possibly overlapping) data decompositions. Once the decomposition is set up, the needed communication schemes can be created automatically and be used to communicate values from containers of various types. Even containers with a varying number of values associated with an entry are possible. In effect, the framework abstracts the decomposition information and the communication in the client code from the eventual parallel paradigm choice.

**Charlotte Herzeel.** presented a case that a programming model is needed in which sequential programs are implicitly parallelized by default, but also offers the flexibility of explicit parallelism on demand. *Controlling Dynamic Parallelization through Layered Reflection* (Charlotte Herzeel, Pascal Costanza, Theo D'Hondt) proposes a layered programming model in which reflective programming techniques can be used to customize the default parallelization strategies.

The authors are currently designing such a layered programming model. As a test case, they are implementing a layered version of a subset of Lisp. In its implementation, loops are parallelized by splicing the different iterations on separate, concurrent threads. To deal with the data races that are potentially created, a dynamic solution based on techniques from software transactional memories is employed. The goal is to provide a reflective interface that makes it possible for a Lisp programmer to specialize this transactional implementation.

The current state of the effort was described, and the initial design ideas, as a position statement, especially with regard their focus on a dynamic compilation instead of static compilation techniques, were presented.

**Francisco Igual-Peña.** As their programmability increases, graphics processors (GPUs) are being increasingly used as computational accelerators for scientific computations. In *Out-of-Core Solution of Linear Systems on Graphics Processors* (Maribel Castillo, Francisco D. Igual, Rafael Mayo, Enrique S. Quintana-Ort, Gregorio, Quintana-Ort, Rafael Rubio, Robert van de Geijn), Francisco Igual-Peña described a tool to develop codes for dense linear algebra operations, with matrices stored on disk, with execution on a GPU. The tool enables rapid development of object-oriented codes, implemented as Matlab M-scripts, for linear algebra operations.

Combined with an implementation of BLAS for a graphics processor, the proposed interface allows the solution of large-scale out-of-core dense linear algebra problems on this class of architectures. The interpreted nature of Matlab code and the usual operation mode of single-precision floating point on graphics hardware introduces penalties that stand in the way of high performance. They described ongoing work including the development of a similar interface for the C programming language and the adaption of the API to new GPUs with double-precision capabilities.

**Olaf Lenz.** Many physical systems of interest are too large to be simulated using classical all-atom molecular dynamics software packages. Instead, *coarse-grained* models are introduced to reduce the number of degrees of freedom and make it possible to simulate such large systems. An increasing number of very different methods for simulating coarse-grained models have been developed during the last decades, for example Particle-Mesh Algorithms or the Fast Multipole Method for electrostatic interactions, Lattice-Boltzmann for hydrodynamic interactions, or r-RESPA for multiple timestep integration, to name just a few. Often, several of these methods must be combined to solve a specific problem. The abstraction and generalization of coarse-grained many-particle simulations is complicated by the great variability of the methods as well as the specifities of certain methods. Therefore, although the increasing complexity of the methods makes it hard for a researcher to implement an efficient, parallelized simulation program from scratch, this is still common practice in the research community.

*ESPResSo* (Extensible Simulation Package for Research on Soft Matter), developed at the Max Planck Institute for Polymer Research in Mainz, Germany, attempted to bridge this gap, and has been successfully applied to many problems in soft matter research. However, the procedural approach of the C programming model proved to be too inflexible to cope with the recent developements in the field.

Olaf Lenz described a joint project of the MPIP and the Fraunhofer Institute for Algorithms and Scientific Computing (SCAI) in Sankt Augustin, Germany, to reimplement the *ESPResSo* software in the C++ programming language. Their system, *ESPResSo++*, a free, open-source, parallelized, object-oriented simulation software system that may be employed to perform physico-chemical molecular dynamics simulations of soft matter systems such as polymers, liquid crystals, colloidal suspensions and biosystems (e.g. biomembranes).

Its open, object-oriented design will give the package the required flexibility to meet the variability of the different methods as well as their specifities, plus the extensibility to cope with future challenges. Furthermore, the design is intended to enable scientists to use *ESPResSo++* as a research platform for their own methodological developments, which at the same time allows the software to grow and to acquire the most modern methods. For maximal freedom, the users will control the program via the object-oriented scripting language Python. *ESPResSo++* is targeted for high performance supercomputers as well as desktop workstations.

**Michelangelo Puliga, Gianni Mula, and Massimiliano Virdis.** presented *The SCORE (Scientific Open Software Repository) Project* (Michelangelo Puliga, Massimiliano Virdis, Enrico Fois, Alessandro Chessa, Andrea Bosin, Gianni Fenu, Gianni Mula). The fundamental motivation of the SCORE project is to make available, for users not strongly skilled in the field of code development or maintenance, a large pool of scientific simulation software. SCORE can be seen as a complement to the well known CCA (Common Component Architecture) approach. In fact CCA, a DOE-funded research project that aims to enable component-based high-performance scientific application development, is very powerful and especially conceived for high performance computing. However, it has proven to be unsuitable for many would-be users because of its high learning curve. This is why, despite much good work, its goal of moving toward a plug-and-play environment for high-performance computing is still largely unrealized.

In contrast, the SCORE project is based on a minimalist approach in which everything can be regarded as a component, provided it can be executed from the command line in a batch-like mode, and no information is needed about its internal structure. Likewise, simulation chains can be built by connecting various components with the use of a glue code that is kept as independent as possible from the internal structure of the components. The extensive use of virtualization technology allows the simultaneous use of different OS's (Linux, BSD, Microsoft Windows) and of different versions of the same software.

As a case study, a tight-binding molecular dynamic simulation was given, stressing the ability of the SCORE approach to encourage code reuse and to foster the growth of a community of scientists who share their stable codes with other researchers. The ability to run even old simulation codes in virtual machine environments, and the provision of standard facilities for community oriented tools (forums, blogs and IM instant messaging) should be further incentives for newcomers to the field to visit its site (www.cybersar.it) and to try the available SCORE project tools.

**Peter Gottschling (1).** Object-oriented software development is a broadly used programming paradigm that is successfully applied to a huge number of large-scale software systems, including many scientific HPC applications. Generic programming, on the other hand, is able to relieve unnecessary interface restrictions, thus allowing for lifting applicability to a potentially infinite number of types. At the same time, conceptual specialization enables algorithmic specialization at compile time leading to optimal performance.

Both paradigms expose many parallels and are simultaneously orthogonal in many aspects. Although their combination does not create a theoretical contradiction, the integration of OO and generic software exposes some technical limitations and is accompanied with several technical difficulties. In presenting *Integrating Object-Oriented and Generic Programming Paradigms in Real-World Software Environments: Experiences with AMDiS and MTL4* (Peter Gottschling, Thomas Witkowski, Axel Voigt), Peter Gottschling demonstrated the relevant problems on the real-world example of integrating the generic linear algebra library MTL4 (Matrix Template Library) into the OO finite element software AMDiS (Adaptive Multi-Dimensional Simulations). Solutions for these problems were shown and the benefits presented in terms of improved generality and increased performance.

**Peter Gottschling (2).** Recursive algorithms, like quicksort, and recursive data structures, like trees, play a central role in programming. In the context of scientific computing, recursive algorithms and memory layouts are studied to provide good cache and TLB locality independent of the platform. With *Generic*

*Support of Algorithmic and Structural Recursion for Scientific Computing* (Peter Gottschling, David S. Wise, Adwait Joshi), Peter Gottschling showed how generic programming and OO allow the abstraction a multitude of dense-matrix memory layouts ranging from conventional row-major and column-major layouts over Z- and I-Morton orders to block-wise combinations of them. All are provided by a single class that is based on their new matrix abstraction.

The algorithmic recursion is supported in generic fashion by classes modeling the new *Recursator*, an analog of the STL iterator. Although this concept supports recursion in general, matrix operations were again the focus. Results were presented for matrix multiplication, on both conventional and tiled representations, using both homogeneous and heterogeneous matrix representations. Reaching about 60% peak performance in portable C++ code establishes competitive performance in the absence of explicit prefetching and other platform-specific tuning. Comparisons with the manufacturers' libraries show superior locality. These new techniques are embedded in the the Matrix Template Library, Version 4 (MTL4).

**René Heinzl.** Techniques for library-centric application design have already proven to be very useful in the past. The current gain in computer performance is shifted towards the utilization of multi-core processors which extends the importance of this type of application design in the field of scalable application design for scientific computing but also poses new difficulties. René Heinzl presented *Parallel Library-Centric Application Design by a Generic Scientific Simulation Environment* (René Heinzl, Philipp Schwaha, Franz Stimpfl, Siegfried Selberherr), describing a parallel generic scientific simulation environment that has been developed to ease the transition from single-core to multi-core systems without additional development effort. They argue that library-centric design not only eases the development of applications significantly by providing building blocks centralized in a generic environment, but also that the evolution of single-processing applications into parallel applications suitable for multi-core processors is significantly supported by parallel components, thereby simplifying development, scalability, stabilization, further support, and parallelization.

**Anton Pegushin.** Intel Threading Building Blocks (TBB) is a C++ runtime library that supports scalable parallel programming for shared memory multiprocessors. The library encapsulates all of the complexity of threading with native threads and only exports a *Task* interface and a set of generic scalable parallel algorithms built over tasks. The user's job is to split the whole application into a set of tasks that can be executed in parallel and the library maps tasks onto worker threads, and in an optimal way: automatically balancing the load, controlling the granularity of the parallelism, and making effective use of cache. By doing so, Intel TBB greatly simplifies parallel programming for application developers and transparently enables support for nested parallelism. Intel TBB is a cross-platform library working on Microsoft Windows, Linux, and Apple MacOS, and is an open-source project, which means that support for other platforms can be added by any member of open-source community. Anton Pegushin gave an overview of TBB's basic functionality: the task scheduler, generic parallel algorithms, memory allocation mechanisms, and concurrent containers. He described in more detail a newly added feature: task cancellation and exception safety. Details of implementation of *parallel-break* for the parallel-for algorithm, and its use cases, were presented.

**Peter Schwaha.** The challenging art of multi-paradigmatic application development, which only few languages currently support, greatly aids the development of highly efficient and reusable software components. Philipp Schwaha presented *Synergies in Scientific Computing by Combining Multi-paradigmatic Languages for High-Performance Applications* (Philipp Schwaha, René Heinzl, Franz Stimpfl, Siegfried Selberherr), describing a link of two such languages, Python and C++, which automatically makes data structures and algorithms realized in C++ using even features such as compile-time meta-programming available to the run-time world of Python. Several generic components and modules for application design in the area of scientific computing were presented. Compile times and run-times were presented to show the proposed combined advantages of both languages. They posited that the employed concepts are not limited to their case study, but are also easily applicable to the wide range of STL standard containers and algorithms, and in particular, for scientific computing.

**Gisela Widmer.** Efficiency is ever of concern in scientific computing. Adaptive methods may reduce actual computational work at the expense of associated overhead. Gisela Widmer explored these tradeoffs in her presentation *Towards an Efficient Object-Oriented C++-Code for Radiative Transfer*. The goal was to design an efficient radiative transfer solver based on the idea of reducing of the number of degrees of freedom in the discretization of the high-dimensional radiative transfer equation. With the sparse tensor product approximation used, the number of degrees of freedom is (up to logarithmic terms) reduced to the number of grid points in space only. However, in order to obtain an overall computational cost that is proportional to the number of grid points in space, special data structures and algorithms, for which no libraries are available, were required. If the sparse tensor product approximation is combined with an adaptive a-posteriori reduction of degrees of freedom, software design for these algorithms is an even more challenging task.

The presentation focused on the a-posteriori adaptive sparse tensor product approximation, where the relevant degrees of freedom are selected in an iterative process, and discussed some key issues for the implementation of the solver, in particular efficient matrix-vector multiplication and preconditioning techniques for iterative solvers.

The advantage of the method is the adaptivity with respect to space as well as solid angle which allows for a large reduction in the number of degrees of freedom for different regimes of radiative transfer. Disadvantages are that the approach suffers from a considerable implementation overhead and many time-consuming runtime decisions.

# 4   An Ongoing Debate

An ongoing discussion regards the appropriateness of a POOSC workshop in general, and the most fitting venues for the workshop.

## 4.1   Continue as a Workshop?

Regarding POOSC as a workshop, there is some sentiment that it could, and perhaps should, grow beyond workshop to full conference status. It is generally understood, however, that some broadening of scope would necessarily be entailed. A subset of the organizers and participants are investigating this possibility. In the meantime, as an annual or biannual workshop it remains successful.

## 4.2   Which Venues Are Appropriate?

To date they have been held at ECOOP with two exceptions: in 2001 a POOSC workshop was held at OOPSLA (Object-Oriented Programming, Systems, Languages, and Applications), and in 2002 at OOPSLA where it was coalesced with JavaGrande.

The essence of the argument is whether the workshop is more appropriate to a computer science/languages conference, or a computational science/software frameworks conference. Some computational scientists present deemed the workshop interesting and worthwhile, but found the ECOOP conference as a whole too far out of field to be of interest. The computer scientists, in contrast, revel in both the content and atmosphere of ECOOP.

One previous participant has since organized a software frameworks workshop at an applied mathematics conference, and this branching is not unwelcome: it provides a venue for those not interested in the *programming language* aspects of parallel object-oriented scientific computing.

ECOOP remains an excellent venue for POOSC. With the discontinuation of JavaGrande at OOPSLA, it may be time to propose it again for that venue as well.

# 5   Conclusions

The POOSC workshop remains an attractive venue for both computer scientists, and to a lesser extent computational scientists, to showcase and discuss their current research, as evidenced by the level of contribution and participation. The field is active, with significant progress being made on numerous problematic fronts, and specifically on many of those enumerated in the call for papers. With the era of new microprocessor architectures upon us (e.g. multi-core, heterogeneous many-core), the need for new and better abstractions, via programming languages and systems, becomes only more urgent.

# 6    Organizers

**Dr. Kei Davis–Chair**
Performance and Architecture Laboratory
Computer Science for High Performance Computing
Los Alamos National Laboratory
CCS-1, MS B287
Los Alamos, NM 87545, U.S.A.
kei.davis@lanl.gov
http://www.c3.lanl.gov/~kei

**Prof. Dr. rer. nat. Jörg Striegnitz–Co-chair**
Fachhochschule Regensburg
University Of Applied Sciences
Faculty of Computer Science and Mathematics
Postfach 12 03 27
93025 Regensburg, Germany
joerg.striegnitz@informatik.fh-Regensburg.de
http://homepages.fh-regensburg.de/~stj39817/people/striegnitz.html

**Dr. Wolfgang Bangerth**
bangerth@ices.utexas.edu
Department of Mathematics
Mailstop 3368
Texas A&M University
College Station, TX 77843-3368, USA
bangerth@math.tamu.edu
http://www.ices.utexas.edu/~bangerth

**Prof. Hans Petter Langtangen**
Department of Scientific Computing
Simula Research Laboratory
P.O. Box 134
NO-1325 Lysaker, Norway
hpl@simula.no
http://www.simula.no/~hpl

**Dr.-Ing. Bernd Mohr**
Forschungszentrum Juelich
Juelich Supercomputing Centre
52425 Juelich
Germany
b.mohr@fz-juelich.de
http://www.fz-juelich.de/jsc/JSCPeople/mohr_b

**Prof. Dr.-Ing. Joerg Nolte**
Chair for Distributed Systems/Operating Systems
Faculty 1: Mathematics, Natural Science and Computer Science
Brandenburg University of Technology
P.O. Box 10 13 44
D-03044 Cottbus, Germany
jon@informatik.tu-cottbus.de
http://www-bs.informatik.tu-cottbus.de/index.php?id=59&L=1

**Dr. Laurent Plagne**
Electricité de France (EDF) Research and Development
1, Avenue du General de Gaulle
BP 408 92141 Clamart CEDEX
France
laurent.plagne@edf.fr

## 7   Workshop Participants

The following reflects the voluntary sign-in sheet and may not include all attendees.

Réza Ansari <ansari@lal.in2p3.fr>
University Paris-Sud

Oved Cohen <oved101@gmail.com>
Israel

Thierry Geraud <theo@lrde.epita.fr>
EPITA Research and Development Lab

Charlotte Herzeel <charlotte.herzeel@vub.be>
Vrije Universiteit Brussel

Olaf Lenz <lenzo@mpip-mainz.mpg.de>
Max Planck Institut für Polymerforschung, Mainz

Gianni Mula <gianni.mula@dsf.unica.it>
University of Cagliari–Cosmolab

Laurent Plagne <laurent.plagne@edf.fr>
EDF France

Ilya Sergey <ilya.sergey@jetbrains.ca>
St. Petersburg State University

Massimiliano Virdis <gianni.mula@dsf.unica.it>
University of Cagliari–Cosmolab

René Heinzl <heinzl@iue.tuwien.ac.at>
Technische Universität Wien

Philipp Schwaha <schwaha@iue.tuwien.ac.at>
Technische Universität Wien

Krzysztof Ostrowski <krzys@cs.cornell.edu>
Cornell University

Markus Blatt <mblatt@gmx.net>
Universität Stuttgart

Gisela Widmer <widmerg@math.ethz.ch>
ETH Zurich

Francisco Igual-Peña <figual@icc.uji.es>
University Jaume I, Spain

Damian Rouson <rouson@sandia.gov>
Sandia National Laboratories, Livermore

Michelangelo Puliga <michelangelo.puliga@dsf.unica.it>
University of Cagliari–Cosmolab

Peter Gottschling <peter.gottschling@tu-dresden.de>
Technische Universität Dresden

Anton Pegushin <anton.pegushin@intel.com>
Intel

# Author Index